MONEY AND THE HUMAN CONDITION

Also by Michael Neary

YOUTH, TRAINING AND THE TRAINING STATE: The Real History of Youth Training in the Twentieth Century

Also by Graham Taylor

STATE REGULATION AND THE POLITICS OF PUBLIC SERVICE: The Case of the Water Industry

Money and the Human Condition

Michael Neary
Lecturer in Sociology
University of Warwick
Coventry

and

Graham Taylor
Lecturer in Sociology
University of the West of England
Bristol

332.4
N35m

 First published in Great Britain 1998 by
MACMILLAN PRESS LTD
Houndmills, Basingstoke, Hampshire RG21 6XS and London
Companies and representatives throughout the world

A catalogue record for this book is available from the British Library.

ISBN 0–333–65959–7

 First published in the United States of America 1998 by
ST. MARTIN'S PRESS, INC.,
Scholarly and Reference Division,
175 Fifth Avenue, New York, N.Y. 10010

ISBN 0–312–21296–8

Library of Congress Cataloging-in-Publication Data
Neary, Michael, 1956–
Money and the human condition / Michael Neary and Graham Taylor.
p. cm.
Includes bibliographical references and index.
ISBN 0–312–21296–8 (cloth)
1. Money. 2. Money—Social aspects. 3. Money—Psychological
aspects. I. Taylor, Graham (Graham John) II. Title.
HG221.N35 1998
332.4—dc21   97–38832
                                                                      CIP

This book is printed on paper suitable for recycling and made from fully managed and sustained forest sources.

10   9   8   7   6   5   4   3   2   1
07   06   05   04   03   02   01   00   99   98

Printed and bound in Great Britain by
Antony Rowe Ltd, Chippenham, Wiltshire

Contents

1 Money Changes Everything...

It is inner space, not outer that needs to be explored. The only truly alien planet is earth.

J.G. Ballard, *A User's Guide to the End of the Millennium* (1996)

Money is the supreme form of social being, yet bourgeois social science makes no investigation into its social life. Economics, the discipline within which such an enquiry might be most expected, remains curiously uninterested, restricting itself to discussions of price, scarcity and resource, allocation, with no specific interest in money as such: 'economics is the study of how men and society choose, *with or without the use of money*, to employ scarce productive resources' (Samuelson, 1967, quoted in Rubin, 1973; emphasis added). Where money is of concern to economists they limit their research to questions about the (dys)functionality of money and its supply.

As for sociology, the discipline within which this book is written, despite its intimate links with classical economics (Parsons, 1951; Parsons and Smeltser, 1956; Schumpeter, 1987), and its preoccupation with investigations into social subjectivity, it has had little to say directly about money. In 1906 Georg Simmel produced the *Philosophy of Money*, but since then there has been little work done on this subject. The sociology of money has been constrained by the limits of its sociological inheritance. Writing inspired by a Weberian interest in social economics has been restricted to an investigation of money in its role as a rational instrument of exchange (Habermas, 1987; Giddens, 1990; Dodd, 1994). Durkheim's version of the importance of money as a 'social fact' is focused on the dysfunctionality of the 'social' without an investigation of the social content of that dysfunction (Ingham, 1996). In poststructuralist accounts, money exists

1

as a discursive equilibrium in the discourses of power (Foucault, 1991); whilst in postmodern accounts its significance is found in its existence as a symbol of everything except itself (Derrida, 1992).

In recent years, however, there has developed an awareness of this deficiency within sociology. As the crisis of Western capitalism has deepened, and the tautologies of its sociological and economic explanations have proved increasingly unable to provide convincing explanations or to offer anything other than intelligent speculations, attempts have been made to combine the disciplines in a way that overcomes their methodological deficiencies. This has included, in particular, a reaction against the methodological individualism, positivism and the functionalism of mainstream economics. This has been done through a sociology which understands economic activity as a form of social action that is socially situated within social institutions (see, for example, the contributions to Granovetter and Swedberg, 1992). But as Ingham (1996) suggests, the signs are not encouraging. The advocacy of the interdisciplinary approach reveals the extent to which current liberal academics are aware of the limitations of each discipline, but the proposal that the limitations of each approach could be overcome through an ecumenical reconciliation avoids the question as to why they should have been separated in the first place.

Modern economics and modern sociology were both derived from political economy in the nineteenth century as denials of the material content of social wealth i.e. *labour*. Modern sociology is based on the same assumptions as modern economics (Clarke, 1991a), both being derived from the denial of the independent interests of the working class. This denial took the form of a political economy organised around subjectivist and individualistic foundations. In economics this took the form of the marginalist revolution. This replaced the classic cost of production theory with a subjectivist theory of value whereby distribution took place, not in terms of the laws of classical economics, but, rather, according to moral and political judgement:

> The rationality of capitalism no longer lay in its dynamic
> efficiency as a system of production, but in its allocative
> efficiency as a system of provision for human needs...
> Marginalism derived the rationality of capitalism from
> the subjectivist rationality of the economic actor.
>
> (Clarke, 1991a: 9)

But the space created by the demise of classical political
economy was not completely filled by marginalist economics.
A discipline was required that could explain non-rational
action or action oriented to non-economic goals. This gap
was filled by modern sociology which developed the notion of
rationality within the same subjectivist, individualist and
rationalised presuppositions as the new economics.

Any reconciliation between economics and sociology
would have to refuse the basis on which they were originally
conceived. In its more enlightened moments, the new economic sociology recognises that these deficiencies and the
concepts of economic sociology they support presuppose
definite social relationships. Ingham (1996) suggests that a
way of overcoming these limitations might be based on forms
of economic enquiry that contain an explicit sociological
awareness. Such an analysis, he argues, is to be found
within a combination of 'heterodox schools': a Keynesian
sensibility, combined with sociology and Marxian political
economy.

Keynesian economics, as Ingham suggests, implies a sociology utilising methodologies outside conventional economics.
For Keynes, economics was 'essentially a moral and not a
natural science... [dealing] with motives, expectations and
psychological uncertainties' (Keynes, 1973: 297). But the
importance of Keynes is not only that he disrupted the cer-
tainty of neoclassical assumptions through the creation of a
sociology of (ir)rational individual expectations within a
macroeconomic generalisation. The significance of his work
to socioeconomic investigation is that he suggested, not simply another sociology for explaining human action, nor
another interpretation of structuralist sociology, but, rather,

that his work contained a sociology of money-capital out of which human action and structural processes are derived.

For Keynes, the primary role of money was to act as a store of value. The significance of this understanding was that, because of the ignorance and uncertainty that characterised economic activity, it was rational for money to be withdrawn from circulation at times when the store could not be increased. This suggested not only that economic irregularities might not be resolved by market mechanisms and would require intervention by the state, but, more fundamentally, it pointed to the deeply contradictory nature of money itself. In order to preserve itself as a store of value money would evacuate the exchange process and thereby precipitate economic crises. This pointed to the influential nature of money, as a form of social subjectivity, in that withdrawals and interventions of money had the capacity of a powerful social force which was able to determine human life and the way in which it was lived. But Keynes did not take this analysis of money any further, nor did he challenge the fundamental nature of capitalism.

The consequence of this was that Keynes was re-assimilated into neoclassical economics as a particular approach to economics rather than as a revolution in economic thought. This re-assimilation was associated with a denial of the idea that the state could regulate the harmonious development of capitalism, and was to be replaced with the notion that only the market had that capacity. The effectiveness of this model relies on the stability of money as an accurate means for the communication of information (e.g. prices) and, therefore, demands a predictable and stable monetary policy. In the pursuit of sound money all else must be sacrificed. Human need is subordinated to the law of money (monetarism).

It is in the area of Marxist theory that the greatest advances in the study of money as an important form of social existence have been most marked. This is not surprising given the centrality of money to Marx's project (Rosdolsky, 1980: 97–166). However, most of the writing on Marx's theory of money has been remarkably sterile, concentrating on the fetishised forms of money as institutional determinations (Aglietta, 1979; Croakley and Harris, 1983), or as a response to the logic of the capitalist system and, therefore, have focused on the formal contradictions of money rather than the contradictions within the system itself (Bonefeld, 1993). Most of these approaches have avoided Marx's important discovery about money: that money is simultaneously both the most concrete and the most abstract expression of the contradictory relations of capitalist production.

In Britain it is through the work of the Conference of Socialist Economists (CSE), inspired by the anti-Bolshevisms of Rosa Luxemburg, Ivan Illich Rubin, Evgeny B. Pashukanis, C.L.R. James and Roman Rosdolsky, that the study of money as a form of social subjectivity is most advanced. This focus on money has developed out of an awareness of the limitations of economics in understanding Marx's theory of value and, therefore, of explaining the basis of the power of capital. The distinctiveness of this debate is the way it presented labour, not merely as the source of surplus-value, but through its understanding of capitalism as the imposition of work through the commodity form. Thus, within capitalist social relations human labour is *forced* to exist as labour-power. Labour can exist only as a form of the wage, as money and through money. In this way money exists 'as the supreme social power through which social reproduction is subordinated to the reproduction of capital' (Clarke, 1988: 14).

The strength of this work is that it has critically examined the bourgeois assumptions of liberal social science, their contaminations in radical sociology, and has exposed the orthodox and crude Marxian derivatives to an immanent critique. It has done this by dissolving the critical categories upon which the bourgeois social sciences and orthodox Marxisms are constructed, without denying either the validity of these categories as empirical realities, or the need to provide a convincing explanation for their social existence. The approach contains an account of the processes out of which these empirical realities are derived, without erecting a new set of absolute categories within which to construct yet further speculation about the real nature of the social world. It is an 'open' critique in the sense that it recognises the closed nature of the theoretical world of liberal social science, whilst refusing to accept that social theory has managed to completely enclose that world.[1]

The social world is not subordinate to social theory. The methodologies of liberal social science and orthodox Marxism reflect the fetishised forms through which social reality exists and is explained. The 'open' account does not reduce this closed world and its explanations to the status of illusions or 'false consciousness', but undertakes to understand and explain the 'thingness' of the thing-like world – a world that is dominated by things and the science of things (liberal social science and orthodox Marxism). This 'open' account recognises the *dialectical* relationship between open and closed, thing and process, content and form, including the practice of theory and the theorising of practice. It recognises the speculative and abstract nature of liberal and Marxist social sciences as a reflection of the abstract and speculative world it is recording. But it does not accept the world in the abstract or the speculative. The 'open' Marxist account is not an abstract or speculative theory, but a theory of abstraction and speculation. There is a real world that can be known.

'Openness' has involved an investigation into the institutional forms of capitalist power and its insubordinations. Determined by the characteristics of power in the modern world the analysis has focused on the state, money and law, opening them up to a new and dangerous world of enquiry, which is neither sociology nor economics, nor even social theory. It is, rather, the immanent critique that exists within these categorisations and which demands to be heard; the possibilities of social life produced in and against the determinations of the institutionalised forms of capitalist power. It is thus a study of class struggle within a determining process. Writing against the liberal interpretations of these structural processes, which exist as unexplained, autonomous levels of functional social intervention, and in opposition to instrumental and structural Marxisms for whom these institutions act on behalf of the ruling class (Miliband, 1969, 1973), or which exist to assure the continuation of the capitalist process (Poulantzas, 1969, 1973), it has defined these institutions as complementary forms of the power of capital derived from the contradictory relationship between capital and labour:[2]

> The underlying unity of these three differentiated and com-plementary forms of capitalist power was explained by Marx's theory of value, the three aspects being united in capitalist property, money representing the most abstract form of capital, whose power is institutionalised in the law and enforced by the state.   (Clarke, 1988: 15)

The theoretical advance of this work is that it explains that which is assumed by liberal social science – the separation between the political, economic and ideological aspects of social reality. It overcomes the crude economic reductionism of orthodox Marxism where the 'economy' is the foundation of all social life – either permanently or in the 'last instance'. It undermines the structural functionalism of bourgeois sociology and it provides a material basis for the power of modern society. Power in the postmodern or poststructuralist sense is thus not the outcome of discourses competing for a hegemonic position, but is derived from the law of money (capital), which defends itself in a range of ways – not least in the form of ideology (e.g. Keynesianism, mon-etarism).

This work has developed to investigate the institutional insubordinations of capitalist power (the working class), in a way that recognises the social subjectivity of labour and its dynamic power within capital. The basis of this dynamic is that workers' demands and capacities are central to the devel-opment of capital. Capital expands through the expansion of their needs and abilities; but, whilst central to the process, the demands and needs of workers are always subordinate to the needs and demands of capital. The power of capital is, there-fore, precarious. It must constantly change its shape and identity in order to contain and exploit the needs and capacities of human labour. A part of this strategy is the avoidance of labour it can no longer control.

This avoidance has been examined in the 'open' Marxist account through an investigation of the way in which capital is forced to evacuate sites of capitalist accumulation and colonise other centres for exploitation. This has taken the form of an analysis of the institutional power of capital expressed as the world market or the global power of capital. The important conclusion from all this work is that the social power of capital is not embedded in any thing (e.g. gold) or in any person (e.g. the capitalist), or in any particular place (e.g. the nation-state), but is derived from the social power of money capital (Clarke, 1988: 17). Forms of social existence, such as gold, the capitalist and the nation-state, merely provide money-capital with a form of social identity and are not the basis of social power.

However, despite the importance of this work, there is one area of social existence that has not been investigated through the 'open' Marxist approach. This most immanent form of critique has avoided the most intimate form of social existence: a theory of the human condition. The Marxist account of the institutionalised forms of capitalist power has investigated the real nature of capitalist power, but not the real nature of human life. In its explanation of the institutionalised forms of capitalist power, it has made no attempt to account for the biographical or psychological character of human life. There are a number of reasons for this, not least the way in which the Frankfurt School introduced psychoanalysis as a substitute for class struggle, or the influence of Lacanian psychoanalysis on Althusserian structuralism against which much of the 'open' Marxist critique is aimed, and the way in which poststructuralism, and in particular the work of Foucault, has become obsessed with the body and the soul. The result has been a tendency for these approaches to accept alienation as a psychological condition rather than for them to situate alienation in the material reality of everyday life.

And yet a science of human biography was central to Karl Marx's project, which he pursued through the concept of *real* psychology:

> It can be seen how the history of *industry* and the *objective* existence of industry, as it has developed is the *open* book of the essential powers of man ... man's psychology present in tangible form; up to now this history has not been grasped in its connection with the *nature* of man, moving in the realm of estrangement, was only capable of conceiving the general existence of man – religion or history in its abstract or universal form of politics, art, literature, etc. – as the reality of man's essential powers and as *man's species activity*... We find ourselves confronted with the *objectified powers of the human essence*, in the form of *sensuous, alien, useful objects*, in the form of estrangement. A psychology for which this book, the most tangible and accessible part of history, is closed, can never become a real science with a genuine content. What indeed should we think of a science which *primly* abstracts from this large area of human labour, and fails to sense its own inadequacy, even though such an extended wealth of human activity says nothing more to it perhaps than what can be said in one word – 'need', common 'need'.
>
> (Marx, 1975b: 354; emphasis in original)

A concern for the real nature of human existence is present in the early works of Marx, if in an idealised form, and is developed later through the concept of commodity fetishism where the abstract 'human essence' of the early writings are given an historical and material basis as a determined form (i.e. human individuality) derived from the social relations of capitalist production. Although Marx was never specific about this adventure in his later works, the search for the secret of human life is present within all his categorical investigations (e.g. class, value, commodities, labour, money, etc.

The presence of human life existing in alienated and perverted forms is present in all of the 'open' Marxist critiques of the closed categories of bourgeois social science, but biographical life is not made the *subject* of any particular investigation. In these studies money is still a remote and inaccessible substance, representing the outer-life of life. The purpose of this book is to investigate the inner-life of money-capital through a *communist science*. It will do so through a concrete analysis of the way in which human life is lived in, through and against its own institutional forms (biography). It is not just the institutionalised forms of capitalist power that exist as forms of capital, but also human life itself, institutionalised as individuated biography and personality. The struggle for human life is not, then, only in and against these alienated forms of power, e.g. in and against the state (London–Edinburgh Weekend Return Group, 1979), but also in and against life itself as biography or personality.

What this book suggests is that there is life in the social universe that has not yet been discovered: sustainable life (communism), now struggling to make contact with itself on an alien planet we call earth – 'the only true alien planet is the Earth'. This planet is becoming more remote and inaccessible as it attempts to escape its formal limits, as is the theory which attempts to explain this process (e.g. globalisation). The purpose of this book is not to follow capital in its attempts to avoid itself as it satellites around the globe, but to confront capital with itself by examining the concrete ways in which life is lived as money-capital and the limitations and possibilities of this human condition.

In chapter 2 I consider in more detail the inability of sociology or economics to understand or explain money. Working with the concept of alchemy, I argue that the explanation of money went underground at the moment that the self-expanding quality of money (capitalism) emerged. Whilst modern economics has got close to discovering the secret of money through the work of J.M. Keynes, it is constrained by its limited ambition and it has been left to Marxism to conjure up money's diabolical capacities. What Marx discovered is that the self-expansive and transforming nature of money-capital is not the result of its own innate potential or the genius of its representatives on earth (capitalists), but is, in fact, the product of the reordering of universal matter through objectified human energy. Money changes nothing. The real 'spirit' of money is alienated labour power.

In chapter 3 I explore the relationship between money and risk through an analysis of the dialectical interplay of the 'law of lottery' and the 'law of insurance' in the development of capitalist social forms. I argue that recent sociological analyses of risk are deficient as they fail to engage with the material crises and contradictions which have made the world a riskier place. It is argued that a principal feature of the development of modern capitalism was an attempt to socialise risks through the subordination of state and society to the laws and principles of the actuary. I explore this through the development of the Keynesian Welfare State which was an explicit attempt to 'plan' the development of capitalism according to the logic of insurance. I argue that the crisis of Keynesianism is simultaneously a crisis of the law of insurance which has resulted in the recrudescence of the 'law of lottery' in the postmodern global capitalist order. This enables me both to posit the emergence of the National Lottery in the UK in a wider historical and material context and to highlight the important relationship between risk and money.

In chapter 4 I examine the 'spirit' of labour power as a processed human form. In modern society human life exists as wage-labour, as a form of money-capital. Human life is constrained by the limitations of money and driven by its possibilities. Money is [anti-] oppressive. I explain this processing as a theory or real psychology (Marx, 1975b), a theory of human personality (Sève, 1975) and schizo-analysis (Deleuze and Guattari, 1977). I argue that this arrangement of human life appeared in the seventeenth century as biography. I examine the concept of biography through the first recorded literary biography, Daniel Defoe's *Moll Flanders*, and as aggregated biography in Peter Linebaugh's social history, *The London Hanged: Crime and Civil Society in the 18th Century*. I suggest that studying human life as a processed form of money-capital (i.e. as a real psychology) opens

for us the possibility of a theory of anti-oppression that is
denied by a metaphysical concentration on ethics, values and
morality. The concrete significance of this chapter is as a
response to current tensions within criminological discourse
and practice in the Probation Service.

In chapter 5 I explore recent attempts to abolish money
through the introduction of local exchange and trading systems (LETS). It is argued that advocates of LETS fail to go
beyond a moral or ethical critique of money, and thereby fail
to grasp either the potential or the limitations of LETS
initiatives. I argue that Marx's attack on the Proudhonists,
who similarly believed that the evils of capitalism could be
overcome via the reform or abolition of money, remains
highly pertinent in assessing the significance and potential
of social movements such as LETS. In particular, I demonstrate the value relations underlying LETS and the way in
which LETS money remains as money in both essence and
form. This is used to highlight the impossibility of true love
or recognition amongst LETS participants, and thus the
impossibility of building real communities on the basis of
LETS networks.

In the final chapter I visit the 'land of the cyborgs' (the
alien planet earth) in order to argue that the infestation of the
world by money-capital has reduced the planet to an alien
place inhabited by man-made machines and machine-made
men. This mechanisation of men and this humanisation of
machines is traced through an ontology of money-capital and
the self. I conclude by arguing for a sustainable form of
human life: communism, which is recoverable from within
the alien world of money.

2 Marx, Magic and the Search for the Secret of Money

Money is the chemical power of the modern world; yet its existence as a supreme social being remains largely unrecognised. This invisibility demands an investigation into its secret life: *an alchemy*. The secret of money has transfixed science, metallurgy, astrology, astronomy, mythology, theology, philosophy, art and magic for thousands of years. Alchemy was the science of the search for the secret of money: the way in which base (iron and copper) and noble (silver) metals could be used to create gold, or the process by which an original quantity of gold could be expanded or *multiplied* – to use an alchemic expression. But alchemy is more than a preoccupation with the transmutation of base metals into noble ones, it was also

> [a] grandiose philosophical system that aimed at penetrating and harmonising the mysteries of creation and of life. It sought to bring the microcosm of man into relation with the macrocosm of the universe. The transmutation of one form of inanimate matter into another, placed in this larger context, was merely an incidental aim of alchemy, designed to afford proof on the material plane of its wider tenets, in particular that of the essential unity of all things.
>
> (Read, 1961: 14)

The purpose of this chapter is to reclaim that alchemic tradition for the modern world.

The history of alchemy is controversial and complex, containing the earliest examples of a fundamental theory of physical science. Thought to have originated in the ancient civilisations that made up the Egyptian, Arabic, Indian, Greek and Oriental worlds, it percolated into Western

Europe in the twelfth century through Latin translations of Arabic texts, one of its earlier translations being Robert of Chester, *The Book of the Composition of Alchemy* (1144).

Although it has a disparate history, alchemy is unified by its principal assumption of the unitary nature of matter (remote); that is, transmutable into other substantial forms (proximate) through a potent transmuting agent: the philosopher's stone – *a motive power*. Originally a substance for turning base metal into gold, the 'stone' later acquired additional properties: the curing of disease or the granting of immortality through 'the elixir of life'. For alchemy, all matter shares the same origin, appearing in various abstracted and separate forms as a manifestation of its essential derived nature. This natural condition is striving in the Aristotelian sense to express perfection and in the Platonic sense to achieve the ambition of its inherent 'goodness'.

The theoretical framework of alchemy is organised within various adaptations: for example, Five Elements (Wu-hsing) and Two Contraries (yin and yang) or four principles or qualities (earth, wind, fire and water). Alchemy maintains that all matter is comprised of these elements in various proportions depending on the tradition. Perfect matter is that within which its elemental form is not apparent: thus gold is the most perfect substance. According to the Aristotelian version these four elements were imbued with a *prima materia*: a quality that had no material existence until it became allied with its form, which allowed one element to transmute into another. Behind these four elements was an other indistinct quality; for Aristotle it was 'ether', the element of the stars; for the neo-Platonists it was 'Logos', or the Word, or God, or Reason. Among medieval philosophy it was known as the *'quinta essencia'*: *the quintessence* (Read, 1961: 3). Alchemy, then, is concerned with the synthetic or induced perfection of matter: the elaboration of a process that occurs naturally in the natural world (Crosland, 1962).

Although it has gained something of a tarnished history, as a confidence trick, or delusion (e.g. Ben Jonson's *The Alchem-*

ist, 1610), it has continued to hold an enduring fascination in philosophy and literature (Goethe, Shakespeare, Chaucer); and an inspiration for esoteric and exotic academic enquiry. It is also gratified by the quality (notoriety) of its various exponents, including all the major intellectual figures of the ancient world: Aristotle, Plato, Copernicus . . . and those who might be attached more comfortably to the modern (e.g. Isaac Newton). Newton's interest in money extended to the practical administration of the Royal Mint between 1696 and 1726 (Craig, 1946); but he was also profoundly interested in alchemy. Newton's 'genius' was completely expressed in his integration of mathematics, physics and astrology; but he also attempted to integrate alchemic ideas with the contemporary mechanical philosophies (Dobb, 1975: xi). In so far as alchemy is concerned, Newton is the last important alchemic adept. (Keynes was very interested in this aspect of Newton's work and collected his alchemic writings and referred to him as the *last magician*.) Newton is the culmination of the process for the search for the secret of money. After Newton alchemy disappears; or rather, it becomes a much more limited endeavour: chemistry.

But this chapter is not an investigation into the history of alchemy in all its esoteric exoticness, or even the history of money. Rather, I take up the quest from the moment that alchemy disappears, when the search for the secret of money is to all intents and purposes abandoned. I shall suggest that this was no arbitrary moment or historical aberration, but that something changes in the nature of money itself which causes it to cease to be a subject for intellectual investigation. Alchemy is abandoned because the inheritors of the modern world (the bourgeoisie), find a way to create money out of money itself. Thus, it is not that alchemy failed to find the secret of money and was, therefore, discredited, but that the search for the secret of money was solved, and in the nature of this practical success the explanation for this solution is obscured. Thus, the discovery of the mystery and its mysterious disappearance as a subject for enquiry are connected.

Money is not ignored from this moment. Theories appear to explain this new phenomenon and the social upheaval the creation of money out of money causes. In the seventeenth century John Locke, a close friend of Isaac Newton, argued against the new world of money (laissez-faire). He argued that a just Godly society is possible only when money is absent. Money is unnatural and against the law of nature, leading to desire beyond need, ambition, beyond morality, corruption and miserliness: 'for as to Money, and such Riches and Treasure... these are none of Nature's goods, they have but a Phantastical imaginary value: Nature has put no such upon them' (quoted in Tully, 1982: 150). However, the theories of money that came to dominate were invested with the naturalness (the rationality) that money seemed to contain, and were concerned, not so much with money itself, but with the system of exchange that money appeared to facilitate: the market and its (dys)functionality. The new theories of money concentrated on monetary policy: the debasement of coin, the prohibition of export in an attempt to determine the real value of money and the control of the problem of price – including, in particular, a debate about the various quantity theories of money (e.g. the debate between David Hume and Sir James Steuart; see Clarke, 1991a and Rubin, 1979).

The most developed modern theory of money appeared in the work of Adam Smith (*The Wealth of Nations*, 1776). The significance of this theory is that it has formed the enduring basis for subsequent economic analyses of money. Smith claimed that 'it is not for its own sake that men desire money, but for the sake of what they can purchase with it' (quoted in Clarke, 1988: 29). His work was opposed to mercantilism, which suggested that the accumulation of money was the dynamic of economic activity, which involved a conceptualisation of money which sought to justify trading and merchant practice. In contrast, Smith sought to assert the instrumental rationality of money, and the system it supports, as a means of enhancing individual and collective material prosperity through a freely developing process of exchange. For Smith, consumption, not accumulation, was the dynamic of economic activity: 'consumption is the sole end and purpose of all production' a proposition 'so perfectly self-evident that it would be absurd to attempt to prove it' (quoted in Clarke, 1988: 29).

Adam Smith naturalised production and consumption within an ideal model of reasonable exchange based on a claimed propensity in human nature 'to truck, barter and exchange one thing for another'. Money – the means through which one thing is exchanged for another thing – becomes a rational device facilitating a rational system, an instrument of exchange and account that enables a barter system to operate effectively and equitably. This system contains its own regulations through its own system of rewards for the thrifty and hard-working, and punishments for the indolent and greedy, with freedom of choice and equality of opportunity for all:

> If money is not an end in itself, but is merely a means of exchanging one thing for another, the powers attributed to money are not inherent in money, but derive from its functions as a means of exchange. The rationality of money is the rationality of the system of exchange whose development it facilitates. Money is the means by which the hidden hand of the market achieves its ends.
>
> (Clarke, 1988: 29)

But in Smith there is no adequate account for the accumulation (expansion) of money as profit, the process by which money makes itself into more money. Following his theory of value, where commodities are exchanged for the quantity of labour they embody, the cost of production or 'constant capital' (machinery, raw materials) resolves into revenue (wages, profit and rent). In this way, the entire product of society goes to the personal consumption of its members. Although Rubin called this is an 'absurd conclusion' (1979: 212–13), this became the dominant explanation of the Classical School: accepted by Ricardo, dogmatised by Say and repeated into the nineteenth century by J.S. Mill. However, the Classical School was unable to account for the expansion of money, for in order to explain the expansion of money it had to abandon the naturalistic premises on which its assumptions were based. That is, it had to acknowledge that the natural equivalence of petty commodity production within which exchange is precipitated by the products of labour is undermined by a society taking on increasing regulatory and administrative forms in response to increasing injustice and disproportionality. David Ricardo came close to making the point that profit equalled unpaid labour, but he failed to develop it. Thus, the Classical School could not account for the continuing expansion of money as wealth and the creation of an employed and unemployed population (Kay and Mott, 1982).

The shortcomings of this theory had been revealed by the end of the nineteenth century when it became obvious that market rationalities (the hidden hand) did not benefit all sections of society. Poverty and its antagonistic forms – socialism – demanded a more convincing account. The new economic theory (marginalism) replaced the rationality of an economic system with the rationality of rational individuals as consumers making informed choices about their own needs as defined by their self-interest. The creation of the rational individual actor is derived from the denial of the independent interest of the working class. This denial took the form of a political economy organised around subjectivist and individualist foundations. In economics this appeared as the marginalist revolution associated with Karl Menger in the Austrian School and Stanley Jevons in the UK. The accounts developed by these economists replaced the 'classic cost' of production theory of value with a subjective theory of value, whereby distribution took place, not in terms of the laws of classical economics, but rather, according to moral and political judgement (Clarke, 1991).

J.M. KEYNES: THE MAGICIAN OF NUMBERS

A revolution in the theory of money appeared in response to the world crisis of money following the world's greatest economic disaster in the 1920s and 1930s. In this period Keynes was formulating an approach to money that was to have decisive importance for the modern world. This 'new' approach owed as much to alchemy as it did to classical economics.

Keynes had been preoccupied with gold as a device for regulating economies, both as a supporter in the case of India in 1913, and as a strident critic against a return to the gold standard for the British economy following the first world war (Clarke, 1988: 204–5). As Robert Skiddelsky has noticed, Keynes was profoundly interested in Isaac Newton and his alchemic experiments. It was only an interest, but one on which he was prepared to spend an inordinate amount of time: 'Newton still absorbs more time than it should; but that is a hobby' (16 August 1936 in a letter to his mother; quoted in Skiddelsky, 1986: 626). Keynes described Newton as 'the last magician'; for Skiddelsky, Keynes was the last magician of number:

> He was not the first of the modern statisticians, but the last of the magicians of number. For him the numbers were akin to those mystic 'signs' or 'clues' by which the necromancers had tried to uncover the secrets of the universe.
>
> (Skiddelsky, 1986: 414)

This is the aspect of Newton that most attracted Keynes:

> He regarded the universe as a cryptogram set by the Almighty. By pure thought, by concentration of mind, the riddle he believed, would be revealed to the initiate.... For some purposes at least, Keynes thought that the distinctions between magic, science and art were less interesting than the similarities.
>
> (ibid.: 414)

Whilst Keynes accepted the conventions of economics, especially the convention of rationality, scattered through his writings are clues to the fact that he regarded the intellectual technique he practised as a surface technique only. He recognised that public life was simply a world of appearance, and that beneath the knowledge in which he dealt there lay an esoteric knowledge open only to a few initiates – the pursuit of which fascinated him as it did Newton (ibid.: 423). Arguing against the laissez-faire principles of classical economics, Keynes maintained that the market system was not self-regulating, it was not clockwork as it had been for Newton. The significance of that discovery is that the market ceases to be the motive power because of difficulties within the nature of money itself. Following Aristotle and Locke, Keynes recognised money as a means of exchange and as a store of value; but whereas they problematised these qualities as leading to an unnatural desire for conspicuous consumption or accumulation of more than one needs, Keynes recognised incipient problems within the relationship between these two functions of money which could be resolved only by extraneous interventions.

The significance of this understanding of the contradictory nature of money as a means of exchange and as a store of value was that, because of the ignorance and uncertainty that characterised economic activity, it was rational for money to be withdrawn from circulation at times when the store could not be increased. Keynes shared this observation with many earlier writers including proudhon and Silvio Gessel (see Mattick, 1971: 5). Keynes argued that if the hoarding of money could be prevented, production and profitability would ensue. This suggested, not only that economic irregularities might not be resolved by market mechanisms and required intervention by the state, but more fundamentally, it pointed to the deeply problematic nature of money itself. In order to preserve itself as a store of value, money would evacuate the exchange process and thereby precipitate economic crises: the declining propensity to consume.

Keynes thus pointed to the influential nature of money itself: money as a means of social subjectivity, whose withdrawals or interventions had the capacity of a powerful social force to determine human life and the way in which was lived. Keynes' alchemic importance, however, is that he discovered the *motive power*, the multiplicatory principle (the notion of the multiplier was an important one for alchemy) through which money could be produced. Through his theory of money, he established the link between the microcosm of man in relation to the macrocosm of the universe; although for Keynes man was still the self-interested actor and his vision of a united universe was restricted to preserving the modern world of the bourgeoisie.

The basis of Keynes magic formula for the expansion of money was *labour*. Keynes recognised the dangers inherent in attempting to reconcile the demands of the working class within the restrictions of the gold standard. Following the First World War and the Bolshevik Revolution he recognised that:

> The labouring classes may no longer be willing to forgo so largely, and the capitalist classes, no longer confident of the future, may seek to enjoy more fully their liberties of consumption so long as they last, and thus precipitate the hour of their confiscation.
>
> (*The Economic Consequences of Peace* [1929] quoted in Mattick, 1971)

Keynes also realised the motive power of this antagonistic subjectivity. Since 1871 state intervention had been on the basis of the working class as the object of the process; but now to accommodate this revealed subjectivity the working class would have to be accommodated on its own terms (Negri, 1988: 12). In an attempt to prevent communism, and to reconcile the demands of the working class within the imperatives of profitable capitalist accumulation, Keynes developed a theory of macroeconomics. This entailed a concentration on money and its aggregate forms (savings, investment, balance of payments and, in particular, wages) as opposed to markets and prices. Orthodox economics argued that lower wages reduce unemployment and unemployment reduces wages, but Keynes maintained that wages were not flexible, workers had learned to defend them. Wages could be reduced more effectively than by trying to cut them. An increase in the quantity of money, linked to extra market policies to ensure 'effective demand', would raise prices and reduce real wages. This could be brought about through the management of mutually independent economic variables. For Keynes, these variables were the propensity to consume and the incentive to invest:

> the wisest course is to advance on both fronts at once ... to promote investments and at the same time, to promote consumption, not merely to the level which, with the existing propensity to consume, would correspond to the increased investment, but to a higher level still.
>
> (J.M. Keynes, *The General Theory of Employment, Interest and Money* quoted in Mattick, 1971: 13–14)

Keynes' solution was profoundly alchemic. It involved the creation of money through a multiplication effect: loan-financed government investment and increased government spending, which would be self-perpetuating and generate resources through taxation and savings to justify the initial deficit. Thus, in order to promote multiplication, it involved the accumulation of induced effects through a manipulation (elaboration) of savings and investments. In this way, Keynes de-naturalised money and explained it as the means of articulating a particular system of social relationships (Clarke, 1991a: 235). But Keynes did not take this analysis of money any further, nor did he challenge the fundamental nature of capitalism. Thus, the nature of the regulation remains incidental, with the purpose of regulation to restore the essential unity of the bourgeois world.

While Keynes created the context within which the motive power of labour could be utilised as a potent catalyst in the expansion of money, his experiment could not control the reaction. The system went into melt-down: *inflation*. This appeared in the 1970s in the form of an economic crisis and the collapse of the post-war boom (Clarke, 1988). Despite his importance Keynes had not fundamentally challenged the basic assumptions of bourgeois economics. The consequence of this was that Keynes was re-assimilated into neoclassical economics as a particular approach to economics rather than as a revolution in economic thought. His alchemic approach was reversed, to emerge as *bad alchemy*, to become not an expansion in the supply of money, but an attempt to control the money supply and to discipline, rather than enhance, the motive power of labour. Alchemy dissolves into a preoccupation with mysticism and metallurgy – *monetarism*. This reassimilation was associated with a denial of the idea that the state could regulate the harmonious development of capitalism. It was replaced by the notion that only the market had that capacity, and that barriers to the smooth operation of the market must be removed. This included the state itself, trade unions, popular democracy, a concentration on supply-side measures, deregulation and privatisation. The effectiveness of this model relies on the stability of money as an accurate means for the communication of information – as prices – and, therefore, demands a predictable and stable monetary policy. In the pursuit of 'sound money' all else must be sacrificed.

SOCIOLOGY AND THE AVOIDANCE OF MONEY

The space created by the demise of alchemy as a search for the secret of money was filled by theories of money concentrating on the market and prices: the formal and symbolic appearance of economic relationships. Whilst this was sufficient to explain rational activity within the limits of the distribution of scarce resources based on individual subjectivity in conjunction with supply and demand, a gap was left that needed to be filled in order to explain behaviour that lay outside this economic relation. This explanation was based on the same, limited assumptions concerning the formal rationality of exchange as had been developed by marginalist economics, and it took the form of modern sociology: the attempt to rationalise the rationality of money as the basis for social action based on non-rational activity. This is evident in classical sociology in Weber's Protestant Ethic, in Simmel's phenomenology of money, and endures through to the structural functionalism of Talcott Parsons and Jürgen Habermas.

In the work of Parsons we find the rationality of a fusion of value (object) and values (subject) in a sociological Keynesian Utopia. Parsons articulates the Keynesian-inspired sociological notion of the subjectivity of money. According to Parsons, money is the rational symbol through which the goals and functions of the constituent sub-systems of society can be both represented and realised. Money ensures that the goods which an economy produces are those that consumers require and allows the state to reward productivity through the allocation of capital funds. Money also encourages entrepreneurial activity through the allocation of profit to innovative firms and individuals (cf. Schumpeter). In this way money constitutes a rational mechanism of communication between the economic and political, ideological and cultural institutions of society.

Habermas attempts to deny this subjectivity. In Habermas we find the rupture of the unity between value (object) and values (subject) and an attempt to ground rationality on an inter-subjective denial of the object (value). This corresponds to the crisis of Keynesian money and money forms. In Habermas's system, power and money are divorced. Habermas rejects the labour theory of value and accepts Weber's theory of the state and political power (see Habermas, 1972). It is this which allows the functional separation of economy, polity and sociocultural spheres in Habermas's analysis of late capitalist society (Habermas, 1988). Money becomes merely an alienated form of 'steering mechanism' which prevents the development of 'communicative rationality'. Money, therefore, is reified as something outside the social relations which constitute the 'lifeworld' and which prevents rational communication. Habermas puts money in a box and allows it to escape only when it interferes with free and equal linguistic exchanges in the mythological sphere of civil society.

This was not a mistake of the classical sociology from which Habermas drew so much of his inspiration – particularly Georg Simmel. Simmel articulated the irrationality of money – although this was articulated alongside the formal rationality of capitalism. Simmel captured the phenomenological spirit of money in his seminal *The Philosophy of Money* (1906), in which he argued that money constituted the essence of modernity, for it was through money that the modern spirit finds its true expression (1979: 429–512). Simmel was concerned with the irrationality of a society dominated by money. This irrationality is attributed to a universal metaphysic or psychological process, premised on the inversion of means and ends and evoked only because money is wrongly designated as the supreme instrument of reason. Money facilitates the objectification of culture through the way in which the division of labour and the development of the money economy creates a specific form of mutual impersonal dependence. The development of the money economy increased individual liberty and individualism, but in such a way that the subjective and objective aspects of life were torn apart. That is, money creates a relationship between individuals whilst leaving individuality outside monetary relationships.

Whilst sociology has recognised the irrationality of money it has simultaneously avoided any confrontation with the content of this irrationality. This has been achieved through the invention of the 'life-world': a sphere in which social subjects are able to escape the objective impositions of money and the state. Sociology has thus tended to *avoid* the contradictions of money. However, as the crises and contradictions of Keynesianism intensified sociological conceptions of money have become increasingly abstract. In the historical context of bad alchemy, sociology has retreated into hyperabstraction – and to present money as merely a simulacrum. Money as simulacrum is the most developed form of the avoidance of the search of money. There is no real money, therefore, there is no real secret. In postmodern social theory, as in all sociology, money is conjured out *intelligent speculation*. Derrida, quoting Mallarmé, remarks on this process as constituting the death of alchemy, what he refers to as the victory of 'sheer intelligence':

A certain deference, towards the extinct laboratory of the philosophers' elixir, would consist of taking up again, without the furnace, the manipulations, the poisons cooled down into something other than precious stones, so as to continue through sheer intelligence.... The null stone, dreaming of gold, once called the philosophical: but it foreshadows, in finance, the future *credit*, preceding *capital* or reducing it to the humility of *money*.

(Derrida, 1992: 116–17; emphasis in original)

Money becomes a sign amongst other signs, but is more than a sign, it is a ghost. Its ghostly appearance is conjured out of the inability of sociology in its structural and post-structural forms to go beyond reciprocity in its analysis of money. Money is only true money when it emerges as the simulacrum of discourse: a sign or symbol. That is to say, there is no way of knowing what is or is not counterfeit, other than the discursive meaning that is imposed on money: 'a true corpus is still perhaps counterfeit money; it may be a ghost or a spirit and of capital' (Derrida, 1992: 97). And Derrida adds that Marx, whom he regards as the chief wizard of money, also fails to penetrate the ghostly apparition of money:

Marx always described money, and more precisely the monetary sign, in the figure of appearance or simulacrum, more exactly of a *ghost*. The figural presentation of the concept seemed to describe some spectral *thing*.... Gold or silver produces a remainder. This remainder is – it remains, precisely – but the shadow of a great name. 'The body of money is but a shadow'. The whole movement of idealization that Marx then describes, whether it is a question of money or of ideologemes, is a production of ghosts, illusions, simulacra, appearances.

(Derrida, 1994: 37; emphasis added)

According to Derrida, Marx was afraid of ghosts. Marx was not a magician content to drive away or exorcise the magic of ghosts with a counter-magic. Instead he attempted to exorcise the ghost through a methodology which counterposed the simulacrum with effective reality – life against death. Despite this Derrida holds that Marx did not actually transcend magic and counter-magic. In other words, Marx was just a magician:

> [Marx] tried to conjure away the ghosts, and everything that was neither life nor death, namely, the re-apparition of the apparition that will never be either the appearing or the disappeared, the phenomenon or its contrary.   (ibid.)

That is, Marx both invented and subsequently denied the simulacrum and the symbolic and ghostly existence of money.

The work of Jean Baudrillard has been central in articulating the apparent pre-eminence of the sign and sign-value in the postmodern order. His work is instructive as is his theoretical starting point in Althusserian structuralism. In his earlier works Baudrillard developed an essentially Althusserian Marxism in order to supplement orthodox Marxism's critique of capitalism with an assessment of the increasing domination of the objects of consumption on individual subjectivity (Baudrillard, 1968, 1970). According to this view, consumption had replaced production as the central mode of homogenisation, alienation and exploitation. Consumption constitutes a higher level of reification through which the 'signs' and 'symbols' attached to commodities result in the total death of the subject by the world of objects (the death of the individual and the social world). The most important form of labour becomes the labour of consuming commodities which allow one to differentiate oneself from others through the meaning, prestige and identity attached to commodities.

The ranking of commodities is achieved through a 'code of political economy' which links sign-value to exchange-value (money):

> [I]t is the code that is determinant: the rules of the interplay between signifiers and exchange-value. Generalized in the system of political economy, it is the code which, in both cases reduces all symbolic ambivalence in order to ground

the 'rational' circulation of values and their play of
exchange in the regulated equivalence of values.

(Baudrillard, 1978: 146–7)

Money is the derivative of the code. The domination of
capitalist society is symbolic. Money has no content other
than symbolic content: it is determined from the abstract as
an abstract form. Money is alienating only in respect of the
role it plays in the symbolic system of meaning represented by
the economic logic of political economy.

The abstraction of money is mirrored in the abstraction of
intellect: money and sheer intellect both serving the highest
and most base needs and desires. The money economy creates
an *abstract* structure or system which reflects back on the
objects from which it has been abstracted – the ghostly apparitions and spectral forms of money. This abstract structure is
constituted by a metaphysical manifestation of objectified
culture which, through the increasing rapidity of 'time–
space compression' (Harvey, 1990) associated with the
money economy, creates an irresolvable tension between
the totality of society and the totality of the individual. As
I demonstrate in the next section, it is through the 'real
magic' of Marx's methodology that the reified apparitions
and ghosts of the world of money can be revealed and
exorcised.

MARX, REAL MAGIC AND THE CRITIQUE OF MONEY

Marx was a magician, but his sorcery was of a different order
from that outlined by Derrida. The reified and fetishised
nature of money is both abstract and real; between life
and death – indeed, a real abstract mediator between life and
death. In denying the possibility of life out of death, post
structuralism articulates the death of money, the crisis of
money – the death of the social – as the subject is objectified
and the object becomes self-referential. The reassimilation of

Keynes into classical economics denies money a subjectivity and so it becomes an object of itself – a ghostly apparition, a simulacrum. The possession of money becomes the most abstract and total expression of individualism, freedom and self-expression and, indeed, a differentiation within the individual: a fragmentation of the self along the myriad of fragmented monetary relations in a generalised money economy. These peculiar characteristics of money make money both a means and an end in (post)modern society, linking all contents of life into a limitless teleological relationship and all relationships expressed in terms of objective exchange.

The problem with this sociology of money in both its modern and postmodern forms is that it conceptualises money as a medium of communication (interaction) and reduces money to a harmless social device with no recognition of its 'orientation to pecuniary acquisition for its own sake' (Weber, 1968: 159). What Weber and Simmel are alluding to but do not develop is the differentiation between money-as-money and money-as-capital. This distinction highlights the problem with poststructuralist conceptualisations of money which fail to recognise the existence of money as anything other than exchange (the spectre) and that 'it is only in the form of money as capital that the limitless drive for the enlargement of exchange-value can turn from a mere chimera into a living, actual reality (Rosdolsky, 1977: 187). For Marx money is a symbol; but it is more than a symbol, i.e. it is a symbol of itself and, in that way, denies its symbolic life. Money is constantly becoming more than itself through its own self-expansion. It is a ghost of something that is not yet dead. Money is living death. Money constitutes a loss of humanity as not-life. Money becomes the ultimate, supreme being:

> Through this *alien mediator* man gazes at his will, his activity, his relation to others as a power independent of them and of himself – instead of man himself being the mediator for man. His slavery thus reaches a climax. It is obvious that this *mediator* must be a *veritable God* since the

mediator is the real power over that which mediates me. His cult becomes an end in itself. Separated from this mediator, objects lose their worth. Thus they only have value in so far as they *represent* him.

(Marx, 1975a: 260–1; emphasis in original)

Human activity (labour) is estranged and becomes the property of a material thing external to man – e.g. money. The cult of money becomes an end in itself. Man has a value only to the extent that he is represented by money (the anticipation of Simmel is startling! But now the important difference). Man becomes money or becomes that which money can buy. Money has magical qualities. Money can conjure intelligence out of stupidity, beauty out of ugliness:

> The properties of money are my ... properties and essential powers. Therefore what I *am* and what I *can do* is by no means determined by my individuality. I *am* ugly, but I can buy the *most beautiful* woman. Which means to say that I am not *ugly*, for the effect of my ugliness, its repelling power, is destroyed by money ... I am a wicked, dishonest, unscrupulous and stupid individual, but money is respected and so is its owner ... Through money I can have anything the human heart desires.
>
> (Marx, 1975b: 377; emphasis in original)

Money, therefore, is a truly creative power. It transforms the contents of the imagination into sensual reality. Without money the demands, passions and desires latent in the imagination remain in the realm of ideas. Needs exist only if there is money to actualise them in reality. As Marx noted:

> money turns the imagination into reality and reality into mere imagination ... real, human natural powers into purely abstract representations and tormenting phantoms, just as it turns real imperfections and phantoms ... into real essential powers and abilities. Thus characterized *money is the universal inversion of individualities*.
>
> (ibid.: 387; emphasis added)

Man (the subject) becomes poorer as the mediator (the thing/ object) becomes richer. Money is omnipotent and the ultimate mediator and objectification of human needs:

> *Money*, in as much as it possesses the *property* of being able to buy everything and appropriate all objects, is the *object* most worth possessing... money is the *pimp* between need and object, between life and man's means of life. But *that* which mediates *my* life also *mediates* the existence of other men for me. It is for me the *other* person.
>
> (ibid: 375; emphasis in original)

Money is the universal confusion of an inverted world. Money is not only contradictory, but makes the contradictions embrace one another. Money is therefore the primordial locus of alienation and reification in bourgeois society. It is, however, the particular *form* that money takes that allows us to see the distinctiveness of Marx's approach. The ultimate achievement of Marx the magician was to expose the mystical appearence of the simulacrum and unveil the subjectivity of labour beneath it. There is a difference between Marx's notion of the abstract nature of money and the concept of simulacrum. A simulacrum is the identical copy of an original that never existed – an abstract abstraction – whereas Marx reveals the material content of the abstraction. He did this through an analysis of labour.

Keynes, as we have seen, recognised the importance of labour as his motive power. But this motivation and its possibilities were limited by his vision of the united universe: the preservation of the bourgeois world. In this sense Keynes was not a magician, but an illusionist, preserving rather than challenging the mystification of capitalistic social relations. Marx, on the other hand, was the real magician; understanding the motive power (subjectivity) of labour and the possibilities for social transformation. His alchemic importance was to recognise that the motive power for the expansion of money lay in the potential that is inherent in the contradiction between labour (as rationality: the unity of need and capacity, i.e. a world without money-capital) and labour-power (as the inability to exist other than through money-capital as the wage, the separation of need and capacity). But not simply labour, the expansion of money lay in the transmutation by labour of one form of matter (nature) into another form (value):

> When man engages in production, he can only proceed as nature does herself, i.e. he can only change the form of the materials. Furthermore, even in this work of modification he is constantly helped by natural forces. Labour then is not the only source of material wealth.   (Marx, 1954: 134)

And in a profoundly alchemic moment Marx adds in a footnote:

> All the phenomena of the universe whether produced by the hand or indeed by the universal laws of physics, are not to be conceived of as an act of creation but solely as a reordering of matter. Composition and separation are the only elements found by the human mind whenever it analyses the notion of reproduction of value . . . and wealth whether *earth, air* and *water* are turned into corn in the fields, the secretion of an insect are turned into silk by the hand of man, or some small pieces of metal are arranged to form a repeating watch.
>
>   (from Pietro Verri, *Meditazioni sulla economia politica* [1771] in Custodi's edition of the Italian economists, *Parte moderna*, vol. 15: 21–2; emphasis added)

What this suggests is that the immanent energy of matter lay within matter itself. Hence, whilst the social power of money appears outside the process of commodity production, and is represented thus by the economists, the motivating energy of this power lies imminently within the money form itself: not as money-as-money, but money-as-capital. Marx formulated the difference between money-as-money and money-as-capital in the equations C–M–C and M–C–M′, where C = commodity and M = money. Capitalist production involves the reproduction of capital or self-expanding value. The basis of this self-expansion is labour-power. In this process money (the general form) and the commodity (the particular form) function only as different modes of existence of capital. Value is, therefore, the subject of this process, changing from one form to another without becoming lost in the movement; but in the process it changes its own magnitude, throwing off surplus-value from itself, and therefore valorising itself independently:

> For the movement in the course of which it adds surplus-value is its own movement, its valorisation is therefore self-valorisation. By virtue of its being value, it has acquired the occult ability to add value to itself. (Marx, 1956: 255)

In this process money is the independent form through which value preserves itself and expands. Money provides value with an identity with which to assert its dominant subjectivity through its process of self-expansion (capital).

Marx discovered the occult nature of money's ability to expand through itself. Whilst money provides value in process (capital) with an identifiable form through which it can expand, it does not imply any change in the magnitude of the value. In the process of exchange (circulation) money functions as the universal equivalent and, therefore, a change of value cannot take place in the money form itself. The change, therefore, can occur only in the use-value of the commodity, in its consumption. It was Marx's major theoretical breakthrough that he identified *the* commodity whose use-value possesses the peculiar quality of being a source and creation of value. The commodity is the capacity to labour: labour-power (Marx, 1954: 270).

It was with the discovery of labour-power (the social form of labour) that Marx was able to postulate the source of surplus-value (the social content, i.e. the alchemic principle). The separation theorised in Marx's early work (alienated labour) is now given a concrete material and socially specific reality and takes the form of the working class as a mass of people separated from themselves (labour and labour-power) and the means of their own survival (the means of production). The perpetuation of this separation is the absolutely necessary precondition for capitalist production (Marx, 1954: 716). It is this relationship of contradiction, antagonism and struggle over production, generalised through reproduction to the whole of human experience, and apparent in the struggle of everyday life, that forms the social basis for the social relations of capitalist society and by which their contradictory nature can be understood (Marx, 1954: 724).

In this chapter I have shown how in the world of money and self-expanding money (capital) it does appear that money changes everything. But as Marx showed, the power of money is conjured out of the alienation of labour. The fifth element, the quintessence of money, is labour. Marx discovered what alchemy did not know: the secret of money. But Marx's discovery was not an esoteric achievement. Marx's magic was real magic. Ernst Fischer in *The Necessity of Art* (1978) defines magic as the domination of nature and the avoidance of work. Through his analysis of capitalist society, Marx explained how the imposition of work through the commodity form (the separation of need and capacity of the working class) could be transformed into a state of abundance (i.e. the unity of need and capacity) and capitalist work abandoned. Thus, the real importance of Marx's magic was to realise that money-as-money changes nothing, it is a ghost, and that the real 'spirit' of money is labour. But in the world of money labour is forced to exist as labour-power: as negative human capacity. The logic of this negative capacity is the domination of nature through *risk* (e.g. nuclear energy and nuclear weapons), the positive capacity is the domination of nature as a state of superabundance (the spectre of communism). In the next chapter I explore the concept of risk in more detail through an analysis of the relationship between risk, chance and the social forms of capital.

3 Risky Business! The Crisis of Insurance and the 'Law of Lottery'

The lottery, with its weekly payout of enormous prizes, was the one public event to which the proles paid serious attention. It was probable that there were some millions of proles for whom the lottery was the principal if not the only reason for staying alive. It was their delight, their folly, their anodyne, their intellectual stimulant. Where the lottery was concerned, even people who could barely read or write seemed capable of intricate calculations and staggering feats of memory... But if there was hope, it lay in the proles.

(*George Orwell*, Nineteen Eighty Four)

There can be little doubt that in recent years life has become increasingly risky. The collapse of the Keynesian Welfare State (KWS) has meant that levels of social welfare and access to employment have increasingly become a game of chance – a lottery. In the UK this national lottery has recently been accompanied by an official version – the *National Lottery*. Risk and chance are thus basic characteristics of the production and reproduction of neo-liberal social formations: positing the economic, political and ideological premises for social reproduction. There is an increasing risk of redundancy or of not being adequately cared for when one is ill, but this is legitimated through a state-sponsored discourse of risk and chance. In other words, the lottery has developed into a social form – a form of social being – which I explore as the 'law of lottery'.

In this chapter I consider the development and role of insurance as a capitalist social form, and the relationship between actuarial risk and the circulation of capital. I consider the way in which the development of Fordism and the KWS were premised on the regulation of state and society according to the 'law of insurance' and the way in which the crisis of Fordism and the KWS is simultaneously a crisis of the 'law of insurance' which has been supplanted by the 'law of lottery'. 'The law of lottery' is connected to the increasing problems of assessing risks through *actuarial principles*, which is itself a crisis of the planner state. I explore this through an analysis of the workings of the National Lottery and the linkages between the crisis of insurance and the crisis of the state. I conclude this chapter through a critique of recent sociological analyses of risk and provide the outlines of an alternative materialist analysis of risk.

THE NATIONAL LOTTERY

There is nothing new about national lotteries. In Britain the first, sanctioned by Elizabeth I, took place in 1569 and consisted of 400,000 lots at 10 shillings each. In the years that followed, the lottery became an essential tool of public finance. The profits from lotteries were used to repair harbours and ports and provided funds for military campaigns: £10 million between 1710 and 1714 to fund the War of Spanish Succession and later over £70 million for the war against the American colonies. The lottery also provided resources for important infrastructural investment: both Westminster Bridge and the British Museum were established with resources from lotteries. The lottery also benefited members of the 'propertied class', who bought vast quantities of the tickets, which were priced at between £10 and £100. These tickets were beyond the means of ordinary people and wealthy agents were able to sell shares in lottery tickets at a premium. This practice was formalised in 1788 when the Treasury sold all tickets to 'lottery contractors' – often stockbrokers – who were responsible for generating the feverish excitement around the drawing of the lottery. Alongside this was the underground practice of 'insurance', whereby individuals could 'hire' a lottery ticket for one of the days on which the lottery was being drawn and were thereby entitled to any prize drawn on that day. There was therefore both the lottery and a lottery within a lottery: gambling on the outcome of the lottery.

The demise of the lottery is often attributed to the wave of public opposition generated by the new generation of political economists. In the seventeenth century William Petty described the lottery as a tax on 'unfortunate, self-conceited fools'. Adam Smith, David Ricardo and Henry Thornton all commented on the negative effects of lotteries on both the moral and economic health of the nation. According to a Parliamentary Report of 1808 the results of the lottery were that:

Idleness, dissipation and poverty were increased: the most sacred and confidential trusts were betrayed, domestic comfort was destroyed, madness was often created, suicide itself was produced and crimes subjecting the perpetrators to death were committed.

This was compounded by the declining proportion of the lottery which contributed to the Exchequer; by 1819 the lottery was contributing less than 1 per cent to the 'ways and means' account of the Government. Consequently, the lottery was abolished in 1823, and apart from premium bonds, which were introduced in 1956, and the football pools (defined as a game of skill rather than chance), it has lain dormant ever since. Indeed, from the Victorian period gambling has been presented by both the state and the Church as a crime and a sin. These attitudes persisted into the twentieth century as can be illustrated by the words of Geoffry Fisher, Archbishop of Canterbury, who, fulminating against the introduction of premium bonds, argued that gambling:

debas[ed] the spiritual coinage of the people [and that] ... the Government knows, as well as the rest of us, that we can regain stability and strength only by unremitting exercise all through the notion of the old fashioned and essential virtue ... honest work honestly rewarded.

(quoted in *Financial Times*, 9 January 1995)

Harold Wilson dubbed premium bonds a 'squalid little raffle'. However, in 1994 the National Lottery was reintroduced, following an absence of over 170 years, with the support of all the political parties and only stifled murmurs of discontent from the established Church. The new National Lottery began operating in November 1994. In its first full year of operation the lottery operated under licence by the Camelot company had achieved sales of £5.2 billion, raised £1.4 billion for various 'good causes' and contributed £677 million to the Exchequer (Camelot, 1996; Fitzherbert et al., 1996). The UK National Lottery is the largest and most efficient lottery in the world, when assessed in terms of the level of sales and as the relationship between sales and contributions to the Government and 'good causes'. Despite odds of 14,000,000 to 1 of winning the jackpot, the lottery attracts 30 million regular players to both a twice-weekly draw and to a variety of scratch cards. Camelot have made great strides to appear as the 'people's lottery' and have invested in extensive 'market research' in order to assess the views of players and to engender a sense of 'ownership' amongst lottery players. Camelot itself has become an important corporate actor: in 1995–6 the company achieved an operating profit of £66.7 million, employed 600 staff and allowed retail agents to earn at least £265 million in extra sales (see Camelot, 1996).

The 'good causes' that benefit from the lottery come under five headings: arts, charities, heritage, millennium and sport. Money is distributed through the Arts Councils, the National Lottery Charities Board, the National Heritage Memorial Fund, the Millennium Commission and the Sports Councils. In deciding on the eligibility of projects for lottery funds, these bodies have to take into account the financial viability of projects, particularly as money is contributed to capital expenditure costs rather than to running costs. With the exception of charities, most grants are dependent on 'partnership' funding from the applicant. Together with the restrictions on local authority capital spending, this has resulted in lottery funds being disproportionately aimed at 'flagship' projects in London and the south-east, whilst the 5 per cent of the population living in the most disadvantaged areas fail even to get a 5 per cent share of funds. In 1995–6 this amounted to 1.7 per cent arts, 1.4 per cent heritage, 3.9 per cent sport, an exception was charities which are directly aimed at this disadvantaged section of the population but still only managed 13 per cent (see Fitzherbert et al., 1996).

As a social form the National Lottery clearly articulates the contradictions of the capital relation. What, however, have been the key historical and logical factors behind its development and increasing importance at the present juncture? Lotteries have become increasingly popular in all advanced societies: indeed, a key argument in supporting the development of a lottery in the UK was that apart from Albania, the UK was the only European state not to have some type of lottery. The National Lottery has played an important role in resolving the fiscal crisis of the state; it represents an ideological form which turns the payment of taxation into a leisure pursuit. The National Lottery is a clear form of voluntary taxation: taxation that is, moreover, highly regressive, with lower earners spending an average of £4 per head as against £1.20 by the better-off (*Financial Times,* 28 June 1995). In a clear link to the past, the fastest sales of lottery tickets have been in the poorest and richest parts of the UK: the devastated council estates of Sunderland and in the Lombard Street Post Office in the City of London (*Financial Times,* 15 July 1995). The state has, in essence, encouraged the expansion of gambling from 74 per cent of the population prior to the lottery to 89 per cent following the introduction of the National Lottery (*Financial Times,* 5 June 1995).

The introduction of the lottery also reveals important insights into the way in which the neo-liberal state has been reconstituted in the UK. The lottery is a new form of *nationalisation.* An intensification of state power which attempts to colonise the worlds of gambling, charity and culture and make them increasingly functional for the neoliberal accumulation of capital. Casualties of this process have been capitals within the UK gambling sector. Following the introduction of the National Lottery, the football pool industry suffered a loss in turnover of between 10 per cent and 15 per cent and Vernons, the second biggest pools operator, suffered a £230 million pre-tax loss in 1994 (*Financial Times*, 11 March 1995). Similarly, spending in the UK's 900 bingo halls has dropped by 20 per cent and the cash pouring into the UK's 210,000 one-arm bandits is £8 million a week less than before the introduction of the lottery. Related to this has been a 17 per cent increase in calls to 'Gamblers Anonymous'. There is also an important sense in which the lottery amounts to an important step towards the nationalisation of culture. Whilst the National Lottery has been presented as part of a 'new cultural golden age' it also will mean the death of many arts organisations which fail to attract lottery funding either because they are not financially viable or because they fail to generate partnership funding. Arts groups will be increasingly dependent on private sector sponsorship to generate partnership finance and this will obviously favour large, commercially viable and mainstream arts groups and projects.

Using the UK as an example, I argue that the regulation of societies through the 'law of lottery' has become increasingly important as the crises and contradictions of the planner state have intensified. In order to understand this process I shall explore the actuarial principles underlying insurance, the way in which these principles underpinned the social form of the Keynesian planner state and how the crises and contradictions of the planner state is simultaneously a crisis of insurance which has resulted in the development and increasing importance of the lottery as a social form.

THE ECONOMICS OF RISK

The category of risk is the fundamental concept underlying the actuarial principles of insurance. The concept of risk was a central concern of classical political economy. According to Adam Smith it is an intrinsic human failing to over-value the chance of gain and hold risk in presumptuous contempt

(Smith, 1970: 210–11). This was evident, Smith argued, in the universal success of *lotteries* through which individuals were systematically encouraged to pay overinflated prices for tickets when the prospective prize was worth only a fraction of the money paid by the total number of subscribers. Conversely, despite the moderate profits and premiums of insurance companies, many individuals held risk in contempt and chose not to insure themselves against potential injury. For Smith, the value of risk amounted to the compensation of common losses and the expenses of management: the profits of insurance being no greater than in other common trades. The level of risk was intimately connected with the level of return to labour and capital (ibid.: 213): levels of wages and returns on stock being proportionate to the hazards faced in their employment in particular sectors. Risk becomes, therefore, the original contribution made by capital in the process of production: the level of reward accruing to labour being a derivative of the level of risk taken by capital (Clarke, 1991: 27).

The unplanned nature of capitalism makes risk a central feature and dynamic in the both the reproduction of capitalist social relations and the continual crisis which threatens the reproduction of these relations. In neo-classical economic theory the category of risk is analysed in terms of the way in which uncertainty is a disutility to marginal maximising individuals. It is a commonplace assumption that the return to capital varies proportionately with the degree of risk to which it is exposed. Uncertainty imposes a cost on 'society' and the removal of uncertainty will be a source of gain (Willett, 1951: 8). Uncertainty is a disutility and will only be borne if something can be gained from doing so. The assumption of risk, therefore, attracts a special economic reward which varies with the degree of uncertainty. Risk is objectified uncertainty and the degree of risk is ascertained by applying the laws of probability to the accumulated results of past events. In this way the utility and disutility of uncertainty allow economic actors to choose between the avoidance, prevention or assumption of risk in particular circumstances.

Insurance is an important means through which uncertainty and the costs which it imposes on capital can be prevented or reduced. Insurance is the 'transfer' of risk to a specialised undertaker of risks in the form of an insurance company. Insurance companies combine and concentrate risks in order to reduce uncertainty and thereby reduce the cost of risk to the wider 'society'. The risk carried by an insurance company is less than the sum of the risks of the insured. The insurance premium makes the incalculable calculable. Insurance constitutes a cost to capital and labour in the sphere of circulation. In the long run insurance is constituted by a 'mutual' insurance fund out of which losses and the costs involved in the provision of insurance are paid by the insured.

> [I]nsurance companies divide the losses of individual capitalists among the capitalist class. But that does not prevent these equalised losses from remaining losses so far as the aggregate social capital is concerned.   (Marx, 1956: 140)

Insurance is the social form through which the losses resulting from the non-valorisation of capital are socialised:

> This is a question of the distribution of the surplus value amongst the different sorts of capitalist and of the deductions which are consequently made from (the surplus value accruing to) the individual capitalists. It has nothing to do with either the nature or the magnitude of the surplus ... Instead of each capitalist insuring himself, it is safer as well as cheaper for him if one section of capital is entrusted with this.   (Marx, 1956a: 357–8)

Insurance constitutes the alienated form in which unexpected losses are socialised in capitalist society. Insurance projects future configurations of time and space on the basis of the past. As time and space are increasingly subordinated to the abstract logic of capital accumulation so they reflect the contradictory determination of all social forms in capitalist society. In capitalist society time and space increasing imply both the possibility and development of not-time and not-space: configurations of time–space outside the circuit of capital. The riskiness of the reproductive cycle of capital accumulation is thus reflected in the social, spatial and temporal representation of insurance as a social form. The crisis of insurance is ultimately a crisis of the rational ordering of time and space on the basis of the capital relation.

THE 'LAW OF INSURANCE' AND THE CRISIS OF THE PLANNER-STATE

In this section I trace the historical processes which link the crisis of insurance to the crisis of the state and the way in which this has resulted in the subordination of the state by the 'law of lottery'. I shall approach this through an exploration of the origins, development and crisis of state insurance in the UK. The origins of social insurance are to be found in the administrative moment of the state. As I mentioned in chapter 1, in capitalist society law and money are the abstract social forms through which the capital relation is produced and reproduced: the creation of formal equivalence through generalised commodity production and exchange by 'free' and 'equal' legal subjects. The state appears as a separate authority to represent the 'impersonal' interests of the system. Capitalist commodity production, however, requires the substantive domination of labour within the labour process and hence the contradictions of capitalism as a social form cannot be totally formalised within the legal and money forms. Alongside formal regulation, therefore, emerges substantive *administration*. The historically specific form of the state is a result of class struggle: the struggle of labour to achieve 'political' gains through the state which escape commodification and which thereby precipitates a process of state restructuring which attempts to reimpose commodification on the production and reproduction of the capital relation.

One of the ways in which labour attempts to escape commodification is through unemployment. This can be either through choice (refusal/crime) or through the anarchy of the market (denial). Either way the potential existence of labour outside the sphere of capital is a threat to the reproduction of the capital relation: highlighting to the working class both the dangers and the possibilities of existing against capital. The problem of unemployment has thus always posed a problem that required *administration*. In the early development of capitalism, marked by the underdevelopment of the socialised worker, the problem could be administered through punitive measures such as the workhouse and poor relief. These forms of administration, however, denied the equality of labour as both workers and citizens, and as the working class developed as a political force, these forms of administration provided the basis for alternative social arrangements based on the possibility of real equality and freedom against capital (communism). It is necessary, therefore, to explore the way in which these developments resulted in the reconstitution of the state on the basis of the '*law of insurance*'.

In the work of classical political economists such as David Ricardo civil society was conceptualised as a 'natural' and self-regulating order of independent labourers. In this approach, the circumstances of the worker were a result of individual decisions taken in the context of natural laws. The conceptualisation of workers as independent labourers was, however, increasingly punctured by the inequality and domination faced by workers in the sphere of production. The abstract regulation of labour needed, therefore, to be increasingly supplemented by the direct and unmediated administration of labour. An attempt to grasp the importance of these changes, albeit in a partial and fetishised way, is provided by the work of William Beveridge on unemployment and insurance.

The work of Beveridge on social insurance was an important moment in the redefinition of poverty and the role of the state in the amelioration of poverty.[1] Beveridge recognised the way in which the development of the working class shattered the apparent naturality of the economy and attempted to demonstrate empirically the factors which constantly forced the labour market away from a condition of equilibrium. The imperfections of the market undermined the independence of the worker. In other words, the market needed administration. An important focus of Beveridge's investigations were, therefore, the causes of unemployment. Beveridge's investigations sought to explore why the laws of political economy had failed to operate and to uncover ways of making them work. The notion of 'independent labourer' could be upheld only if workers were rewarded for behaviour and character congruent with the morality of money. Beveridge was thus concerned to create administratively the conditions in which the morality of the 'independent labourer' could be rewarded. Beveridge deepened the concerns of classical political economy through the way in which the 'independent labourer' was made both a premise and goal of political economy. In policy terms the labour exchange was to administer the relationship between the supply and demand of labour. In the context of a socialised working class the surplus population could not simply be discarded as Ricardo had done: political economy needed administratively to create and maintain the conditions for the existence of the 'independent labourer' and to adequately differentiate between these independent and dependent workers.

The 'discovery' of poverty and unemployment was inextricably tied to the potential for socialism. This is the context in which social insurance was developed. Insurance recognised the potential of the working class against capital, and attempted to reincorporate the working class through the administrative reconstruction of the 'independent labourer'. The system of social insurance established by the Beveridge reforms was premised on a state-administered compulsory insurance scheme which *socialised* the risk posed to the integrity of the 'independent labourer' by the poverty associated with unemployment, and thus a state-administered 'collective wage' replaced the individual wage. The efficient administration of this process was premised on the accurate calculation of likely levels of unemployment and thereby politicised these levels through their transformation into an administrative category. The discretion inherent to the administrative moment of the

state, therefore, posed both a threat to the actuarial sound-
ness of the system and threatened to deepen the crisis of the
liberal form of the state.

The 'law of insurance' was necessarily mediated by the
abstract social forms of money and the law. The monetary
relationship was premised on the contributions paid by the
worker and the asymmetrical relationship between benefit
and the wage. The system was to be 'policed' by making
benefits dependent on genuine 'need' and the punishment of
malingerers and fraudulent claimants. In order for social
insurance to work it was necessary for the state to calculate
the level of unemployment accurately in order to balance
contributions and benefits. The administrative discretion
inherent in state insurance as a social form, however, allowed
the state to cover higher than expected levels of unemployment through general taxation. Social insurance, therefore,
linked aggregate levels of unemployment to the fiscal crisis of
the state. In other words, insurance became a form of class
struggle. Throughout the 1920s and 1930s the working
class in the UK struggled over the form of insurance: a
struggle for ad hoc benefits and against the means test.
Where it was politically expedient – as in 1919 when ex-
servicemen and munitions workers were granted extra benefits
in order to quell potential revolt – levels of benefit were
indeed increased through administrative intervention.

The development of the welfare state thus resulted in the
Ricardian 'law of nature' being replaced by the 'law of insurance'. The abstract premises of the actuary were, however,
constantly ruptured by the concrete development and movement of the working class, and Beveridge himself conceded
that during the 1920s the actuarial basis of the state insurance
system was never adhered to (Beveridge, 1930: 277 quoted in
Dixon, 1996). The development of the 'insured worker' forced
the organising principle of the insurance scheme from contract to status: benefit linked to classes of claimants rather
than to the contribution of benefits. The crisis of insurance
was ultimately addressed by Keynes who devised a way of
setting levels of unemployment by the state.

As I mentioned above insurance makes the incalculable calculable through the way in which it projects future configurations of time–space on the basis of the past. Through the political establishment of an aggregate level of unemployment, Keynes allowed the future to be projected on the basis of a recognition that the working class could be maintained only if the subjectivity of labour could be tied inextricably to the development of capital in its most abstract and inscrutable form – *money*. This required the further administration of money through fiscal and monetary policies which regulated the money supply in order to provide levels of benefits and services demanded by labour through the representative channels of the KWS. The 'law of insurance' was thus dependent on the monetary stability provided at the global level by the Bretton Woods agreement and the subsequent global hegemony of the dollar and the stable administration of money domestically by the nation state.

Keynesianism thus provided a way of socialising and thus controlling risks inherent to capital accumulation at the global level. Paradoxically, however, this was a highly contradictory and risky strategy for capital to undertake. The law of value cannot be suspended through administrative intervention because the capital relation on which the law of value is premised is not a thing but a *social relation*. The state is a political form of this relation and is thus unable to resolve the contradictions on which it is premised as a social form. The state is premised on the coexistence of the circuits C-M-C and M-C-M' and the provision of administrative goods and services through the circuit C-M-C is necessarily mediated by the forms of abstraction inherent to the circuit M-C-M'. The crisis of the capital relation, therefore, became increasingly manifest as a crisis of the state. The state provided welfare and social insurance, but in alienating and oppressive forms designed to contain the costs of administration within the socialised valorisation imperatives of capital. The working class demanded reforms to the social welfare system through the extension of benefits and the reform of provision. The 'law of insurance' was thus the historical manifestation of class struggle in the postwar period.

The internal decomposition of Keynesianism was eventually compounded by a global crisis of overaccumulation engendered by the contradictions inherent in the administration of global money by the IMF and the World Bank. The crisis was resolved through the restructuring of capital and the state through the ways in which the administrative and political forms of Keynesianism were (re)subordinated to the abstract power of money and law. The temporal and spatial configuration of capital became liberated from place and the result was a global intensification of capital accumulation and the neo-liberal restructuring of the nation-state (Burnham, 1996). The intensification and globalisation of capital has made the actuarial calculation of risk increasingly problematic. The state no longer has the *dirigiste* mechanisms to maintain aggregate levels of employment and the spatial and temporal impact of unemployment has, therefore, become a matter of *chance*: a lottery. The 'law of insurance' has thus been supplanted by the *'law of lottery'*.

The neo-liberal restructuring has involved the simultaneous restructuring of the economic, political and ideological aspects of the capital relation. The political deconstruction of the institutions of the welfare state and the economic deregulation of the market has thus been accompanied by the development of an ideological focus on chance and risk. The National Lottery is the most developed institutional form of this process. Against the certitude of protection from ill-health, unemployment and poverty is the chance of abject poverty or untold virtues. The crisis of state insurance is thus part of a wider crisis of capital as the intensity of change and the increasingly massive risks faced by humanity make the calculability of the future increasingly problematic.

THE SOCIOLOGY OF RISK AND THE RISKS OF SOCIOLOGY

As Anthony Giddens has rightly argued, life has always been a risky business. He continues to question why risk and assessments of risk have become so significant in modern societies (Giddens, 1991: 29). Modern sociology has explored the increasing importance of risk through an exploration of the ways in which individual and institutional reflexivity facilitated by the development and intensification of modernity open up the space for counterfactual thinking and action. The debate between modern and postmodern sociologies has hinged on the ontological status of reflexivity: cognitive or aesthetic. Within sociology the dominant approach has been to present risk as an ontological category which develops through a 'reflexive' project of the self. The abstract premises of this approach, however, precludes a rigorous assessment of the role of real (abstract) processes, such as capital accumulation, in the constitution of the self: the way in which individual conceptions of time and space develop in a dialectical relationship to the restructuring of time and space by material social processes. In other words, the complex and contradictory relationship between 'object' and 'subject' inherent to social forms of capital.

The 'cognitive' approach to 'risk society' has been developed by Beck (1992), who is concerned with the self-conscious project through which the dangerously modern social world, the catastrophically normal 'risk society', might recreate itself as a sustainable modernity. He combines a postmodern denial of the rationality of scientific endeavour (scientism: 'modernisation': industrial society) – which he sees as a not yet completed process responsible for the creation of previously unconsidered dangers, risks and arrested developments beyond compensation in the form of ecological disaster, disruptions of work, gender, class and political relations – with an historically informed Habermasian enlightened logic. This casts off the pessimism of Adorno, Weber and Foucault and provides for a modernity developing beyond its industrial design. Through a cognitive political sociology, he argues that the creation of this 'risk society' creates its own ethical critique (security), the rational is rationalised through a process of existential biographical reflection driven by the inadequacies and dangers inherent in the scientific process. He

describes this critical, customised, self-consciousness as reflexive modernisation: a condition of being, determined by
consciousness (knowledge). The realm within which this consciousness thrives is not the gaseous test-tubes of the laboratory, but the democratically neurotic, ambivalent, anxious
and pragmatic managed institutions of civil society.

The focus on 'risk' as a central mediation in modern processes of cognitive reflexivity is also a feature of the recent work
of Giddens (1990, 1991). Risk and uncertainty result from the
restructuring of time and space by the dynamic processes of
modernity. Modernity is marked by the development of
'abstract systems' or 'disembedding mechanisms' which result
in a process of 'time–space distanciation': the separation and
abstraction of time from concrete space. These abstract systems include 'symbolic tokens' such as money and expert systems such as the state. These abstract systems are the processes
through which time and space are organised and constantly
reorganised and form the basis of the subjectively defined
'trust' and 'ontological security' of individual social actors. In
the 'globalised' and 'intensified' state of 'high' or 'radicalised'
modernity the unpredictable and unforeseen consequences of
modern development undermine trust in 'expert systems' and
make 'risk' and 'risk assessment' the centrally defining feature
of individual subjectivity. Increasingly, the 'future' is perceived
actuarially in terms of counterfactual possibilities. In a similar
way to Beck, Giddens highlights the way in which counterfactual discursives form the potential for social movements to
recapture control over future configurations of time and space
through 'utopian realist' political projects.

The 'cognitive' conceptualisation of reflexivity and risk has
been challenged by Lash and Urry (1994), who argue that in
'late' or 'post-' modernity reflexivity takes on an increasingly
'symbolic' or 'aesthetic' form. Lash and Urry argue that the
'cognitive' approach to reflexivity results in the polarisation
of subject and object, which ignores the self-referential nature
of reflexivity alluded to by writers such as Mauss and Bourdieu, and the importance of the 'symbolic' and the 'allegor-
ical' in the construction of (post)modern social subjects. Time

and space are 'emptied out' of their material content and Cartesian configurations of time–space become subjective and symbolic time–space. The city becomes either an 'urban heterotopia' or emerges as a source of subjectively defined moral affectivity and the basis for the fragmented symbolic struggles of new social movements. Time is emptied of its concrete 'Taylorite' and 'Fordist' content and becomes discursively defined by flexible and subjectively oriented forms of post-Fordist production and consumption. Lash and Urry argue that these forms of (post)modern aesthetic and symbolic reflexivity have potentially liberatory potential by opening positive 'life-spaces' for individuals in all spheres of social existence. While the (post)modern world is risky, therefore, risk is an inherently empowering and liberating process.

The strengths of Beck and Giddens are that they attempt to recover the political power of human activity driven by rationalised needs and capacities. The weakness is that their work is founded on an idealist premise which detaches political power from economics and economics from society.[2] In this way it conflates the normative rational assumptions of bourgeois social science with the alienated (irrational) capitalist forms within which human sociability is expressed. Whilst Lash and Urry highlight the potential for struggle and opposition against the constantly crumbling edifice of capitalist social forms their foundationless relativism nevertheless celebrates the irrationality of these forms. This occurs through a conflation of value and values – between capital and the self.[3] This cannot be repaired by subjecting the source of this alienation: capital, to a Beck-like critique, as Rustin (1994) suggests; but can only be deconstructed by an immanent critique not simply of risk, but of the concept of modernity itself.

THE MATERIALITY OF RISK: HISTORICAL AND LOGICAL DETERMINATIONS

I shall conclude this chapter through the elaboration of an alternative materialist analysis of risk. I will approach this with reference to the reproduction schema presented by Marx in *Capital: Volume Two*. The dynamism and the contradictions underlying the development of the modern condition is premised on the contradictory coexistence of the circuits C-M-C and M-C-M'. The latter is an inherently risky process as far as capital is concerned. In the metamorphosis of capital through its successive forms – money capital, productive capital, commodity capital, (more) money capital. M-P...C -M' – time and space are constantly ruptured and there is constant risk and uncertainty with respect to the (re)structuring of time and space in a way which permits the successful accumulation of capital. The process is ruptured by the necessary social reproduction of labour through the wage (money) form (Marx, 1956b: 35). The unfettered subjectivity of labour is denied by its necessary reproduction through the wage form: money advanced through the wage to enable labour access to commodities necessary for their own reproduction (L-M-P). Hence:

> *The risk faced by individuals in everyday life is thus the alienated and fetishised form in which the risks attendant on the reproduction of capital appear.*

In the (post)modern world 'risk fetishism' is the sociological accompaniment of commodity fetishism. The 'actuarialisation' of society is the ideological expression of the risks faced by capital in the neo-liberal process of global capital accumulation.

The crisis of insurance is thus a *crisis of private property*. A crisis of private property becomes a crisis of the most concrete form of private property: *money*. A crisis of money becomes a crisis of money's most abstract form: *capital*. A crisis of capital becomes a crisis of the law and its enforcement: the *state*. A crisis of the state demands a more concrete imposition of capital through its most concrete form: the enforcement of the law of money through poverty in an attempt to moralise the demoralised, and through bigger risk to offset bigger disaster. The imposition of poverty and bigger risk becomes a crisis of insurance (more crime, bigger disaster). The state can no longer protect the social relationship out of which it is derived and expressed as private property. Vigilantes are required to enforce poverty. Bigger risk lies beyond the world of quantifiable redemption!

Insurance makes the world a safer place for capital. Insurance predicts the risks to future patterns of spatial and temporal development on the basis of the past. The increasingly intense and globalised circuits through which capital flows has made prediction increasingly problematic. Indeed, the rational, capitalistic ordering of time–space has reached the limits of its contradictory form. This is the crisis of insurance. The increasingly uncertain nature of the future makes the quantification of risk increasingly difficult. It is important to recognise however that capital is not a 'thing' or a 'symbol' but a *social relation*: a relation premised on the subordination of living labour power to the abstract power of money capital. The crisis of insurance is thus a crisis of the reproduction of labour as labour-power in the circuit of capital accumulation. The crisis is manifested in many forms: crime, ecological disaster, nuclear Armageddon... The material manifestation of the risk society is thus a generalised crisis of *uninsurability* expressed through the 'law of lottery'. The death of the future – how soon is now?

4 Probation, Criminology and Anti-oppression

THE CURRENT PREDICAMENT

The Probation Service of England and Wales is the least spectacular agency within the Criminal Justice System (CJS), lacking the dramas and cruel tensions of other aspects of law enforcement. Working in the space between the Courts, the Police and the Prison Service, its practice is motivated by a commitment to the principle of social justice, involving a concern for the well-being of all those caught up within the administration of the law, including, and, in particular, the people against whom the law is being enforced ('the offender'). In recent years this 'decent' presence has been questioned as the Probation Service, along with other parts of the CJS, has been forced to redefine itself in response to the social difficulties experienced by all western democracies and the associated rapid escalation of crime (May, 1994).

This realignment in the administration of crime initially through the Criminal Justice Act (1991), offered the Probation Service a central role in the management of recidivism, but has more recently, through the repeal of the 1991 Act by the Criminal Justice and Public Order Act (1995), driven the Service to the point where it is barely recognisable even to itself. Decency and discrimination are being replaced by a managerial authoritarianism (May, 1994; Nellis, 1995).

In response to this punishing imposition, and in an attempt to protect itself, the Probation Service and its scientists are developing a set of values through which they can defend and develop their work. In opposition to the new reactionary realism displayed by the Home Office, the Probation Service intelligentsia is formulating its own realistic set of proposals, now being worked out in a debate between those who wish to reaffirm the general principle of social justice based within a

55

commitment to liberal individualism (to reaffirm the Service's traditional role) and those who argue for a more practical, realistic and precise definition within the same moral arrangement. The advocates of this approach argue that the social justice ethic, and its attendant social work practice is ill-defined, that it fails to take into account the new reality of management within the service (i.e. 'benevolent corporatism') and calls for a more criminologically sophisticated value-base built around the linked notions of anti-custodialism, restorative justice and community safety so as to redefine the Probation Service as a Community Justice Agency (Nellis, 1995).

Despite the humanitarian and apparently radical aspect of these proposals they are deeply problematic. Mainstream criminology suffers from its normative assumptions: morality is assumed as a basis for human action, with crime an egotistical deviation. The exercise of sanctions is legitimated through recourse to a supra-social and ahistorical secular, metaphysical authority. Radical social science (critical criminology), despite its more material foundations, is also inadequate as a theory for progressive social transformation. It dogmatically assumes that crime functions as the ideological support to a system of social control within which criminality is romanticised as the logical consequence. Mainstream criminology is deficient because it concentrates on the form of social power without an investigation of the content out of which this form is derived. Radical criminology is inadequate because it concentrates on the content of social power: its repressive character, without explaining why these precise forms of regulation exist in the form that they do. It is left to imply that punishment follows some rational logic of repression with no clear understanding of how these repressive instruments can be transformed (Fine, 1984).

The problems inherent in these positions have meant that the debate has got bogged down as both sides search for the ethical high ground, or try to demonstrate their ability to reflect more accurately the reality of the present situation by ever-more pragmatic solutions. In the meantime the whole project is undermined by an escalation in criminal activity and an ever-more reactionary political response.

The purpose of this chapter is to intervene in this debate and to open up new areas for discussion. I take as my starting point remarks made by Mike Nellis (1995), who in a perceptive aside points to the poverty of theoretical interpretation within this debate and the need for a theory that counters the repressive regimes that the Probation Service is forced to take up:

> The more fundamental concept of anti-oppressiveness can be revised to produce new ways of thinking about probation values . . . anti-oppressiveness is a serviceable basis for further arguments . . . anti-oppressiveness has not been adequately theorised, and until such work is done its intellectual foundations will remain precarious.   (ibid.: 30)

In order to advance this debate Nellis cites the work of Paulo Friere and Erich Fromm; but, having set up this interesting channel for discussion, he abandons it and, avoiding the problem, escapes back into mainstream and critical criminology.

It is precisely my intention to ground this debate within a theory of anti-oppression. I shall contextualise the discussion within a political philosophy that argues against the current dominant bourgeois orthodoxies in a manner that is logically, historically and materially informed. Following Nellis's advice, I shall situate the discussion in the world of anti-psychology with an investigation into the work of Erich Fromm and other writings in the anti-psychological tradition (i.e. Lucien Sève, Deleuze and Guattari). From Lucien Sève, I take it that a theory of anti-oppression must include a theory of human personality, i.e. an investigation not simply of the will to power (state); but an autopsy into the will to life, the 'science of human biography', as Sève has it. I shall show how Deleuze and Guattari have developed this theory of personality through an exposition of Marx's theory of money and of history. I support these abstractions through an examination of two ways in which the emergence of money as a supreme form of social power has been recorded: as the novel and as social history. In *Moll Flanders*, Daniel Defoe, writing in the eighteenth century, gives an account of the first biographical life. In *The London Hanged: Crime and Civil Society in 18th Century London* (1991) Peter Linebaugh provides a social history of money through the aggregated biographies of the London poor. From this work, I shall conclude that (auto)-biographical life is a life lived as a human processed form of the social relations of capital. I shall substantiate all of this by way of another historical account of the Probation Service and with reference to my own biography.

PAULO FRIERE

Nellis reminds us that Paulo Friere is one of the few genuine radicals to have influenced social work practice; and, therefore, despite the fact that he has disappeared under the onslaught of radical management theory, we would do well to rediscover his work. The strength of Friere's work is the obviously successful campaigns to develop literacy in Latin America. However, although the subversive nature of his analysis has proved an inspiration to radical educationalists and excited the fears of the Brazilian generals in 1964, who jailed him for 70 days following the military coup, it is limited as a theory on which to base anti-oppressive strategy. Friere's theorising suffers from a complete lack of concrete or material analysis.

While his work derives out of a sympathy for the real condition of class oppression imposed on the Brazilian poor there is no explanation for the logic of that oppression other than as a left version of a standard theory of political elites, whose position is psychologised as an oppressive motivation explained by the rulers' ambition to remain powerful. This is linked to a Maoist attachment to revolutionary education as an aspect of cultural transformation within an idealist notion of the Hegelian dialectic. His recourse to psychoanalytic theory is superficial, borrowing from Fromm and Marcuse without any reference to their considerable theoretical disagreements. His suggestion that the poor form an attachment to an enlightened cadre, who will provide them with the intellectual tools to understand the nature of their predicament and how to transcend it, has obvious appeal for academics already in positions of authority. However, its validity as a theory of revolution has been undermined by the Chinese nightmare of the cultural revolution in the 1960s and the degradation of revolutionary movements in Latin America, i.e. into Castroism and Guevarism.

ERICH FROMM

A more rewarding area for investigation can be found in the work of Erich Fromm (1900–80). Working within the problem of consciousness, and searching for an explanation for human behaviour, Erich Fromm formed part of the tradition of radical psychoanalysis – including Wilhelm Reich, the Frankfurt School and the Surrealists – that attempted to explain, following the Freudian moment (1856–1939), human behaviour as a science of the irrational or the theory of the unconscious. That is, Fromm sought to combine Marx's class theory with Freud's theory of instinctual drives.

Fromm took from Sigmund Freud the assertion that 'most of that which we are conscious of is not real and that most of what is real is not in our consciousness' (Fromm, 1971: 14). It was, therefore, the unconscious (the hidden) that held the key to real desire, expressed concretely as dreams, neurosis and 'unintentional' acts. For Fromm it was no longer sufficient to explain human activity simply from behaviour or intention, rather it was necessary to analyse what lay behind it. The progressive aspect of this theory of human irrationality (psychoanalysis) was that through an awareness of the psyche, one can understand and control irrationality (i.e. self-destructive tendencies) through Reason. The negative aspect was that, for Freud, needs and desires are constant, their satisfaction was an end in itself.

Fromm argued that this satisfied formulation denied Freud any revolutionary potential. Fromm exposed the bourgeois assumptions that underpinned Freud's work and the politics that it supported. Freud's notion of repressed sexuality was derived from his own notion of society as the ultimate form of human organisation. In this way Freud becomes part of the intellectual bourgeois project reflected in other liberal social science, e.g. Weber in sociology and marginalist economics (see Clarke, 1991a). In the psychoanalytical moment man is the abstract individual of bourgeois economics, isolated, self-sufficient, realising his needs through exchange in the market which appears to work for the mutual satisfaction of all. Driven by the economic notion of scarcity, man is motivated by the desire to satisfy his need for self-preservation (the reality principle) and sexual satisfaction (the pleasure principle).

The reactionary tendency of this theory for Fromm was that within the Freudian theory of need man is driven by the necessity to unburden himself of unpleasurable tensions. It denies the possibility of a theory of need as a result of abundance where human behaviour is not driven simply by the need to survive within the limits of that society; but, rather, to desire more intense human experience. Although Fromm accepted that Freud had produced a dynamic reading of human action, he argued that Freud destroyed the dynamism in his model by converting the social and historical into a timeless myth: a Greek tragedy. Man might be striving to make sense of his life, but his life is already scripted.

This script takes on ever more tragic dimensions with Freud's reassessment of the nature of man following the horrors of the First World War. Ego and sexuality are subsumed within a notion of the life instinct (Eros) in opposition to the death instinct (Thanatos), the root of all human destructiveness. This new configuration abandons any possibility of human satisfaction, carrying the notion of the avoidance of unpleasure and tension to its ultimate place of complete unstimulation: death. Destructiveness is inevitable. Death reduces the tension of social life completely, returning living substance to the 'quiescence of the inorganic world' (Fromm, 1970: 47).

Fromm developed his understanding of consciousness through the work of Karl Marx. In the *German Ideology* Marx wrote: 'It is not consciousness that determines life, but life that determines consciousness'; and in the Preface to *The Contribution to the Critique of Political Economy*: 'It is not the consciousness of men that determines their existence but, on the contrary, it is their social existence that determines consciousness.'

In order to establish this connection between psychoanalysis and historical materialism, psychology and sociology, Fromm premised that all social phenomena are related back to relations between human beings which had somehow escaped from human control. Following the Marxist humanist tradition, found in Lukács and the early work of Marx, Fromm sought to investigate the 'social totality' rather than just its economic base. Fromm's radical Marxist social psychology was constructed on the basis that it was necessary to investigate the social world from a perspective of the fundamental nature of the mode of production and the class-based nature of society. Central to Fromm's concern was the acceptance of the notion of individual and personal gratification and development as against the Freudian notion of repressed individuality. Fromm, therefore, rejected Freud's libido theory, the Oedipus complex and the biological determinism of instinctual theory.

Fromm rediscovered Marx's interest in psychology, 'the natural science of man' (Marx, 1975b: 354). Unlike Freud and liberal social science, Marx does not deal with man as abstraction. Marx's concept of man is dynamic: driven by passion and desire in relation to that which can satisfy. These drives are not ends in themselves, nor are they the product of animal instincts or chemistry; they are social, the energy through which man transforms himself and the world around him. Man does not simply use the world to satisfy his desire, but expresses himself in and through the world. The limits and possibilities of this process are explained in Marx's theory of alienation. For Marx, sensuality is the active expression of human reality, and man's ability to confirm himself in this relation. Each new recognition opens up a new possibility of development: 'each new object truly recognised opens up a new organ within ourselves' (Fromm, 1970: 67).

Fromm's work is important. It points out that the inability to overcome the impossibilities of everyday life is not simply a crisis of psychoanalysis, nor even a crisis of man, but a crisis of life itself. And that within this problematic, psycho-analysis still has a crucial role to play because it deals with issues of 'critical awareness, the uncovering of the deadly illusions and rationalisations that paralyse the power to act' (ibid.: 191).

But despite the importance of these insights, it is not at all clear how helpful they are in developing a real material psychology or a theory of anti-oppression, or to what extent he escapes the necrophiliac eschatology of Freud, or the idealistic and moralising tendencies in Marx's early work. In *Escape from Freedom* (1941) the spontaneous inspiration required to develop truth and social justice is introduced as an extraneous variable rather than the product of a specific social relation. His notion of 'social character' suffers from social-psychological functionalism. He tends to socialise psy-chology and psychologise the social (Wiggerhaus, 1994: 272–3). In *The Art of Loving* (1957), a treatise informed by eastern religions, Spinozian philosophy, Freud and Marx, Fromm's pertinent understandings about the nature of modern love are undermined by a romantic mysticism. And, finally, revolution is conjured up by a supranatural appeal to the transcendental mysteries of creation: 'In the name of Life!' (Fromm, 1957: 192). In order to develop a real material theory of anti-oppression we need to look elsewhere.

LUCIEN SÈVE: A THEORY OF HUMAN PERSONALITY

An attempt to continue this analysis and develop it more materially can be found in the work of Lucien Sève. Writing in 1968, Sève's project was to develop a theory of personality, the absence of which he suggests is a problem not just for psychology but for all social science. The development of a theory of personality requires a radical philosophical and political critique (materialist and dialectic) of psychology's basic concepts; to expose and understand its own limited terms of reference and, in particular, to highlight psychology's ambitious but confusing concept of man: the study of human behaviour.

Sève refers to psychology's working notion of its object of enquiry as the 'logical monstrosity' that undermines all psychological investigation. All psychology presupposes a particular philosophy of man. It understands that human personality is premised on the belief that the individual personality is a particular example of the general personality, that the concrete individual is a single variation of man in general, but man in general can be nothing other than an abstract individual. In order to overcome this contradiction, psychology seeks refuge in the speculative pseudo-materiality of biology (in which social life is naturalised) or the idealistic pseudo-scientificity of sociology (where particularity is re-generalised as ideal-types and categories), and/or a combination of both. Sève argues that the behaviourist focus abandons the social relations or the determining conditions within which human personality is developed. He gives the example of wage-labour where the condition within which the activity of workers is determined is ignored and wages become the preoccupation of the economist.

Sève finds a more compelling basis for a real psychology in the work of Karl Marx, not only in his early writing on the subject where he deals specifically with psychology, but also more usefully when the speculations of this early work were immanently developed through his theory of commodity fetishism. Through this work Marx replaces his earlier concept of abstract man or 'human essence' with a theory of abstraction where the substance of man is found, not in his individuality, but within the ensemble of real-life processes (social relations) which man produces and which produce him. It was Marx's project to discover these processes so that he might more adequately conceive of a scientific theory of personality. This investigation, argues Sève, took forms that were not always psychological, but the question of the real nature of man is present in all the categories that Marx examined in his later work (e.g. abstract and concrete labour, money, surplus value, the general law of capitalist accumulation...). Sève suggests that there is no short-cut to this project: any attempt to base a real psychology on the early work leads back to a speculative humanism (cf. Fromm). Such is the nature of the project that it has not been completed. The project began by Marx has not been set back on its feet. Sève suggests a way forward by the integration of historical materialism with what he calls 'the science of human biography' (Sève, 1975: 39), within which every form of human existence has at once its characteristic social relation and its specific form of human individuality.

Sève argues that the relationship between the form of specific individualities is an immanent one. For example, Marx's categories of capitalist and worker are not basic personality types but the objective logic of the activity out of which they are derived: the capitalist as 'capital personified' and labour as 'a machine for the production of human value'. In this way, the particularity of each concrete individual, each biography, is the result of the process in and against which it is produced. Each life can then be analysed in relation to a series of acts considered in the context of their objective social results (psychology). This Sèvian concept of acts is a much more dynamic idea than the more orthodox notion of human behaviour. It is based on a progressive idea of human need, or what Sève calls, 'the expanded reproduction of activity'.

Sève develops this idea through an exposition of the central yet subordinate position of humanity in the process of capitalist accumulation, through a discussion of the relationship between need and desire, production and consumption. The Freudian thesis is that the fundamental motor of human activity is the reduction of tension or the fulfilment of a desire: that needs are satisfied through consumption. Sève argues that this exposition fails to explain the expanded reproduction of activity or 'the appropriation of a social heritage'. Sève suggests, following Marx's theory of capital valorisation,[1] that the expansion of human need and desire is produced from within the circuit of capitalist (re)production: desire is valorised. This demonstrates not only the social and historical character of human need, but also, at the same time, demonstrates the central yet subordinate position of human existence in the production of itself.

This argument has devastating consequences for liberal social theory and orthodox Marxist account of class struggle for whom the working class exist as a fetished category. It suggests that as a form of capital (wage-labour) human life exists against itself. The struggle against oppression, therefore, involves a struggle in and against the form through which human life exists and not just against an external alienated form of capitalist power (e.g. the state).

ANTI-OEDIPUS

This hypothesis is elaborated further in *Anti-Oedipus, Capitalism and Schizophrenia* (1984) written by Gilles Deleuze and Félix Guattari. In this book they develop a theory of anti-oppression (revolution) through what they claim is a material psychiatry against the repression of psychoanalysis and its Oedipalised object. Central to the theory, and in common with others examined so far in this anti-psychoanalytic movement, is the notion of desire as a process of self production in a society of abundance. What is important for my analysis is that Deleuze and Guattari locate the problem of desire and repression through Marx's theory of money-capital and the development of revolutionary theories of money in the work of J.M. Keynes:[2]

One of Keynes' contributions was the reintroduction of desire into the problem of money; it is this that must be subjected to the requirements of a Marxist analysis. That is

why it is unfortunate that Marxist economics too often
dwell on considerations concerning the mode of production, and on the theory of money as the general equivalent
as found in the first section of Capital, without attaching
enough importance to banking practice, to financial opera-
tions, and to the specific circulation of credit money –
which would be the meaning of a return to Marx, to the
Marxist theory of money.

(Deleuze and Guattari, 1984: 230)

Deleuze and Guattari develop Marx's concept of the relation between man (social) and his world (nature), expressed in
the *Economic and Philosophical Manuscripts*, the *Grundrisse*
and *Capital*. For them man exists in an immanent relationship with the world. Man is not simply the bearer of a
relation or an appendage to the machine. Man is the relation.
He is the machine. There is nothing else. Within Deleuze and
Guattari's cybernetic universe, machines and the logic of
machines (production) have replaced man and nature; nothing else has any meaning, everything is production, everything has the same essential reality, with desire as its
immanent principle, its divine energy, dissolving all idealistic
and normative categories. This process is driven, not by
Platonic lack or Oedipal need or Kantian fantasy, but by
passion, defined as 'the essential reality of man and nature',
or 'the missing subject'. For Deleuze and Guattari, to talk of
a fixed subject is always to talk of repression. What is real is
what is produced: 'There is only desire and the social and
nothing else' (Deleuze and Guattari, 1984).

BODY WITHOUT ORGANS

For Deleuze and Guattari, the process of production within
which man and nature have been subsumed is deeply problematic; it suffers from organisation. This takes the form of
identity, abstraction and the not-consumable. Deleuze and
Guattari formulate this organised condition as the 'body

without organs'. In a conceptualisation that reworks Marx's notion of commodity fetishism, they argue that this organisation regulates and records production as a process of anti-production. That is, the 'body without organs' forms the surface of this process and provides the identity on which the process is recorded and distributed. It claims what appears to be the case, that the process emanates from it, as a miraculated form of its own, non-derived power, or a 'true consciousness of a false movement'. The false movement is apparently derived from the movement of that which provides its identity, abstraction and not-consumables: money. The modern form of the Body without Organs is then the Body of Money: 'the fluid and petrified substance of money, for it will give the sterility of money the form whereby money produces money' (Deleuze and Guattari, 1984).

What makes the Body of Money different from previous bodies without organs (The Earth Body and The Despotic Body) is the nature of capitalist production. The Body of Money does not simply regulate and record codes which are inscribed upon it, but decodes and recodes the codes as they come up against their own limit. Capitalism then operates by decoding flows, that is, substituting for intrinsic codes (i.e. codes that have an internal logic [e.g. community]) an axiomatic code of abstract quantities in the form of money. Deuleuze and Guattari argue that this process of (expansion), of concreting the abstract, of decoding, occurs through the form that money takes: as wages and as finance:

> In the one case impotent money signs of exchange value, a flow of means of payment relative to consumer goods and use-values, and a one to one relation between money and an imposed range of products ('which I have a right to, which are my due, so they're mine'); in the other case, signs of the power of capital, flows of financing, a system of differential quotients of production that bear witness to a prospective force or a long term evaluation, not realisable *hic et nunc*, and functioning as an axiomatic of abstract quantities. In the one case, money represents a potential

break-deduction in a flow of consumption; in the other case, it represents a break-detachment and a re-articulation of economic chains directed toward the adaptation of flows of production to the disjunctions of capital.

(Deleuze and Guattari, 1984: 228–9)

This dissimilation provides the ground for the immanence of the social relation of modern society and provides the dynamic for the logic of desire. One money flow works within and against and through the other:

> The apparent objective movement where the lower or subordinate form is no less necessary than the other ... and where no integration of the dominated classes could occur without the shadow of this unapplied principle of convertibility – which is enough, however, to ensure that the desire of the most disadvantaged creature will invest with all its strength irrespective of any economic understanding or lack of it, the capitalist social field as a whole. Flows, who doesn't desire flows, and relationships between flows, and breaks in flows? – all of which capitalism was able to mobilise and break under these hitherto unknown conditions of money. (ibid.: 1984, 229)

In this process society and all forms of life are monetised:

> A global object of an investment to desire. The wage earners desire, the capitalists desire, everything moves to the rhythm of the one and the same desire, founded on the differential relation of flows having no assignable exterior limit, and where capitalism reproduces its immanent limits on an ever widening and more comprehensive scale. (ibid.: 239)

Negative desire, or the capacity for man to appear to desire repression (Fascism), is not the product of ideology, of false consciousness, but the result of real material flows: 'a secret investment of desire', which is contained within the monetisation of society. This is a material process. Production is real. It is 'at the level of flows, the monetary flows included, and not at the level of ideology, that the integration of desire is achieved' (ibid.: 239).

The way in which money flows, and its connection with desire, is theorised by Deleuze and Guattari within Marx's theory of money: C-M-C (payment) and M-C-M' (financing). Capitalism can only proceed by continually developing the subjective essence of abstract wealth or production for the sake of production, that is, 'production as an end in itself, the absolute development of the productivity of labour'; but on the other hand and at the same time, it can do so only in the framework of its own limited purpose as a determinate mode of production, 'the self-expansion of existing capital':

> Under the first aspect capitalism is continually surpassing its own limits, always de-territorialising further, displaying a cosmopolitan, universal energy which overthrows every restriction and bond; but under the second, strictly complementary aspect, capitalism is continually confronting limits and barriers that are interior and immanent to itself (desire), and that, precisely because they are immanent let themselves be overcome only provided they are produced on a wider scale.   (ibid.: 259–60)

Capitalism, therefore, liberates the flows of desire, the worker is free to sell his labour, wage-labour takes on an equivalence or a demand that needs to be satisfied: desire, 'a generalised decoding of flows'. However, this occurs under the social conditions that define its own limit and the possibility of its own dissolution. The condition of wage-labour needs to be enforced, freedom and equality are imposed as Oedipus. The Body of Money is constantly opposing with all its exasperated strength the movement that drives it towards its schizophrenic limit:

> The moment when capital comes face to face with itself and the limits of its own mortality: its inherent tendency brought to fulfilment, its surplus product, its proletariat and its exterminating angel.   (ibid.: 35)

This is a contradictory process, coding and recoding social existence, between paranoia (the state), schizophrenia (the limit of the condition), and celibacy (the celibate machine), the way in which the process might be transcended. For Deleuze and Guattari the celibate-machine is the opposition between the desiring machine and the body without organs. This opposition produces a new form of humanity, i.e. it contains traces of the previous way of existing but is essentially a new form of existential reality. Everything about it is different (Deleuze and Guattari, 1984: 18). What is new and different is the fact that it can only exist as, through and against money. Human life loses its dependency on other humans and gains a new dependency on money. Human life becomes the possibility of an independent life. The human condition loses its immediate connection between other independent lives and the world around it and is suspended in a condition of permanent desire, or a 'zone of intensity' that can only be satisfied through the agency of money (Deleuze and Guattari, 1984: 18). As this agent of satisfaction is alien to human life consummation is always a degraded and degrading aspiration (Tomkins, 1997).

Deleuze and Guattari propose *schizo-analysis* as a theory of anti-oppression, as a material psychology to counteract the repressive nature of Oedipus, to answer the question why people appear to desire their own repression. And, at the same time, to explain what motivates revolution. Schizophrenia is not revolutionary; the process is schizophrenic. Capitalism is mad. Society is not driven mad; it is mad. Schizo-analysis expresses the contradictory manner in which life exists, as the economy of desire and the desire for economy. In the former, it exists as the unconscious libidinal investment of desire, i.e. to introduce a new code, to realise its molecular possibilities: revolution. In the latter it exists as the preconscious investment of class or interest enslaved to a structured molar aggregate, anti-revolution or the revolution betrayed (e.g. social democracy). Each form of desire is realised through the form of money-as-capital; in its subordination as wage-labour desire invests passionately in the system that oppresses it; and as capital, creating the desire that will ultimately consume itself.

MONEY: ITS LIFE AND TIMES – A MARXIST HISTORY

This thesis can be supported by an analysis of the development of money as a submissive object of desire into a mass weapon of its own destruction. That is, through an examination of the creation of what we now call 'society', the process through which the social world became monetised in the seventeenth and eighteenth centuries. This historical moment is the culmination of a process of decomposition of feudal authority that had been going on since at least the twelfth century. Feudal authority had not been constituted by one dominant logic, but by a constellation of order that tended towards, but did not demand, a unifying principle. Under feudal regulation law was based on custom and tradition, with rights and privileges appertaining to concrete individuals or a delimited group of individuals. Each town, estate or guild had its own traditional rules, with no common universal legal status common to all. Each regulation was particular and local (guild, estate, etc.), each relation was personal and visible, each instruction was private and direct. This was an immediate political system of disorder predicated on absolute authority; each relation was a relation of power, of personal domination and subordination. It was a situation of extensive inequality (Kay and Mott, 1982).

The economic condition of the later middle ages (from the twelfth to the fifteenth century) was restricted to regional economies based on the town and the countryside. Within this system a substantial portion of peasant production was for their own consumption, another part of their production (not money) went as rent (established by custom) and another part of a peasant's productive life was in the service (*corvée*) of the appropriate lord. What meagre surpluses were made by peasants were sold at market, the money made was used to buy tools from urban craftsmen in a process of production that was regulated by the customary demand and monopoly regulations. Any surplus production accumulated by the lord was sold or bartered for luxury items from home and abroad. What is important to note is the fact that the rural feudal economy was distinguished by its overwhelmingly *natural* character and the feeble development of money exchange (Rubin, 1979: 19).

By the sixteenth century this system was being dissolved through the decomposition of the natural economy under the pressure of a money-economy and the growth of merchant capital. Merchant capital is based on the principle of buying cheap and selling dear. In the monopoly and protected markets this enabled merchant traders to accumulate vast amounts of wealth. At the same time, colonial development saw an enormous increase in the amount of precious metal and an improvement in the extraction technologies. This ensured a rise in the quantity of money in circulation, leading to an increase in commercial exchange, and fuelling the demand for yet more money. Faced with this pressure of the growth in the importance of money feudal landowners abandoned the quick rent system in favour of the creation of rented free ten- ancies, which went to the highest bidder. Peasants were expelled from their land to which they had a customary right, to create room for grazing sheep, whose wool had become lucrative in the expanding international market:

> Gentleman do not consider it a crime to drive poor people off their property. On the contrary, they insist that the land belongs to them and throw the poor out from their shelter, like curs. In England, at the moment, thousands of people go begging, staggering from door to door.
>
> (Thomas More, *Utopia*, p. 23)

The law was used to deprive people of their customary rights and to drive them into the expanding production process in the towns. That is, to force them to exist as wage-labour, to exist through money. The penalty for refusal to work, 'vagabondage', was brutal:

> The measures adopted by the state against vagabondage were harsh: able bodied vagabonds were lashed or had their chests branded with red-hot irons; persistent vagrants were liable to execution. At the same time maximum wage rates payable to workers were established by law. The brutal moves against vagabondage, and the laws setting maximum wages were attempts by governments of the day to turn these declassed social elements into a disciplined obedient class of wage workers who, for a pittance, would offer up their labour to a youthful and growing capitalism.   (Rubin, 1979: 24)

In the towns this process of decomposition of the feudal economic order was occurring through the insertion of money into the process of production. What were regional economies were now being connected through the universal value of money. These connections were made through the deliberate creation of surpluses by producing commodities to be sold in the new demanding and rewarding (inter)national markets. This market was facilitated by the appearance of 'middlemen' with orders that needed to be satisfied. The significance of this is that the direct link between producer and consumer is broken. There is now a logic external to the previously self-serving economy. Initially these 'middlemen' bought a portion of what was being produced, but eventually demand expanded to the point where they were buying the total volume produced. Eventually, a position is arrived at where the 'middlemen' are giving producers orders, supplying them with the raw materials and paying them a remuneration (the *wage*). The wage turns the independent craftworker into a dependent wage-earner. This process develops as cottage industry, machino-facture and eventually as the factory with a highly developed division of labour.

The significance of this process in so far as money is concerned is that money has taken on a new social identity.

Money is not simply a rational instrument of exchange, it is now, as money-capital, money that exists in order to make more money through the process of production – the determining logic of the whole productive system. Money-capital now exists as the supreme and unavoidable social power. Money now has two identities: it is *schizophrenic*.

These two functions of money are essential aspects to the development of the capitalist system. Surplus-value is produced in the process of production and realised in exchange. But these two functional identities suggest different logical imperatives. As a rational instrument of exchange, money is the means by and through which human need is satisfied; enabling humanity to exist as independent choosing beings and, therefore, as moral individuals. As money-capital exists in order to make itself more, it has no interest other than itself. In this form it is indifferent to human need. It is *cruel* and *brutal*.

Political economy has focused on one or other of these identities. For Adam Smith money, as a rational instrument of exchange, could facilitate human happiness. For Karl Marx money, as money-capital, could lead only to eventual human immiseration. The value of money-capital can expand only by forcing labour into wage-labour and keeping the value of labour low. If anything threatens the expansion of value, it will evacuate that place leaving a trail of destruction in its wake.

The process through which this monetisation of social life occurred was one of extraordinary upheaval. The seventeenth century is the most revolutionary period in English history, featuring regicide after the Civil War; the establishment of a Republic under the Protectorate of Oliver Cromwell; Restoration, when the Old Order tried to reassert itself; and finally Revolution in 1688, when the Old Order was reconstituted as the monetisation of society (Hill, 1991). This moment is described in orthodox history as the reconstitution of the monarchy in a form we know today, answerable to Parliament and having only limited powers. In fact, the whole of society was reconstituted. This moment was the culmination of six hundreds of years of struggle, and witnessed the transition from the religion-based ethics of feudalism to the secular ethics of capitalism. It was a period when the traditional controls were removed; right and wrong were to be negotiated; the Divine Right of Kings became the Divine Right of Providence. Property became King (Mitchell, 1978: 10).

This period saw the reconstitution of the whole of society at all levels. The ground-rules and explanations of everyday life had to be redefined:

> Thus the period is one of profound value confusion and of unusual social, economic and morality mobility – the like of which has not been seen since in England. It was a time of great uncertainty when different moral and legal codes conflicted in their claims to universal validity. It was a period when the values which today we hold as self-evident were very much up for grabs... the clear cut oppositions of crime and good citizenship, morality and immorality... have not yet separated themselves out.   (Mitchell, 1978: 10–11)

This is a period when what we now know as the criminal law was struggling to establish itself. Fewer people were punished for their religious or political views. The rapid escalation in the number of crimes that incurred the death penalty was for crimes against property: 'capital' punishment. Despite the disorder of this period its significance for criminological study has rarely been fully understood (see Thompson, 1977; Hill, 1991; Linebaugh, 1991). The transition from feudal to capital relations has been portrayed by the bourgeois social sciences as an evolutionary development based on the rationality of historical progress around improved technology of industry and agriculture. However, this narrative entirely misses the point. What is being struggled over in this period, following the intervention of money-capital into the process of production, is a new form of existential reality (see Rubin, 1979). As Christopher Hill (1991) has it: 'The world was turned upside down.' It is impossible to underestimate the significance of this upheaval, nor the problem that this new reality had in invoking and reconstituting itself as a political society. What was at stake was nothing less than the basis of human value and of human life.'

In order to understand this upheaval, it is useful to look at the way in which the new social order – 'society' – recorded the process. And the way in which it attempted to understand itself through the novel, a new art-form that appeared at this time.

DANIEL DEFOE

Moll Flanders, written in 1723 by Daniel Defoe, but set in 1682, was one of the first attempt to record this new social order. The book is a dramatisation of the conflict and confusion that occurred in the seventeenth century over the establishment of a new moral and legal basis of capitalist society. Juliet Mitchell, in the Introduction to the 1978 edition, argues that the novel endures as 'a profound consideration of the creation of social values and the relationship of the individual to society' (Mitchell, 1978: 5).

The story is the first story of a life lived: the first biography. It begins with Moll as an orphaned child of 'criminal' pedigree; it traces her sexual adventures, including incest, marriage and prostitution, and her decline into crime – at which she was very successful. It records her punishments, her escapes and her eventual triumph into a prosperous old age. Through an account of the monetisation of society, it provides an account of the first appearance of human life processed as a form of money.

Money is among the main protagonists in the novel. Money is the reason Moll does anything and provides her with the capacity to do anything. Moll steals and is a prostitute for one reason: she has no money. When prosperous, she leads a moral life. Moll exists as a juxtaposition of contradictory moral elements which have been imposed on her through the monetisation of the social world. She is heroine and villain, capitalist and thief, wife and prostitute, saint and sinner. Mitchell (ibid.) makes the point that the boundary between crime and non-crime is hard to draw at this moment and that 'the epoch in which she lived was still struggling to convince itself of the distinction'. This problem of 'distinction' applied not just to a definition of crime but to all aspects of social life including and especially the nature of the relationship between the sexes and the precise nature of human nature.

Making the same point, but from the detached perspective of a social history, Peter Linebaugh considers the phenomenon of human lives as they are lived through the development of the monetisation of society. In order to draw general conclusions about the period, the policy and its criminal behaviours, Linebaugh uses the technique of aggregating biographies (i.e. the consideration of groups of individuals, 'the London Hanged', studied as individual dramas). Aggregation, he argues, enables us to understand the similarities and differences between the condemned and the condemning, and to consider that what may appear incidental or anecdotal in the individual case may attain from an aggregated study a significance that puts it close to the essence of class relations in civil society.

In *The London Hanged: A Critical Study of Hanging in the 18th Century* Linebaugh investigates this most terrible sanction through a conceptualisation of money-capital as the determining social condition:

> In criminology as in economics there is scarcely a more powerful word than 'capital'. In the former discipline it denotes death; in the latter it has designated the 'substance' or the 'stock' of life: apparently opposite meanings. Just why the same word 'capital' has come to mean both crimes punishable by death and the accumulation of wealth founded on the produce of previous (or dead) labour might be left to etymologists were not the association so striking, so contradictory, and so exact in expressing the theme of this book. For this book explores the relationship between the organised death of living labour (capital punishment) and the oppression of the living by dead labour (the punishment of capital).
>
> (Linebaugh, 1991: xv)

Inspired by E.P. Thompson, George Rudé and E.J. Hobsbawm, who investigated the history of premodern crime (e.g.

Robin Hood), and developing themes explored in *Albion's Fatal Tree* (1975), Linebaugh provides a history of crime and punishment in the eighteenth century through a social history of money.

Periodised chronologically to correspond to stages of capitalist development (finance capitalism, mercantilism, manufacture and industrialisation) and written within the traditions of economic history, rather than any discussion of the theories of money, Linebaugh investigates lives lived in response to the increasing monetisation of society through the imposition of wage-labour (urbanisation) and the struggle of the labouring poor to resist such an imposition (urban crime). He argues that the method of payment for workers or their employers was so sporadic within this system that crime becomes the way in which unpaid labour exists in a monetised society, and corruption the way in which the ruling class acquired their surplus; so that crime and corruption are endemic in the system itself. Crime is not a pathological condition of the individual: the individual is a product of the monetisation of society (Moll Flanders); it is not an 'anomic' condition arising from a sophisticated division of labour (Durkheim): the division of labour is the result of the introduction of money into the process of production. It is not the result of the culturally inspired will to over-achievement denied by structural incapacities, but the nature of monetised society itself. It is not a cultural phenomenon, or even a category of drift. It is much simpler than that: the hanged belonged to the labouring poor.

THEORY OF ANTI-OPPRESSION: PROBATION

The struggle within human biography occurs in and against the institutional forms of organised power (the state). The Probation Service as a form of state power is a part of this oppression. This struggle can be examined historically through an investigation of its developing forms. The history of the Probation Service is usually presented as an historical accident, developing out of an encounter between the Temperance Movement's Church Court Missionaries and the drunken, criminal classes of the late nineteenth century (Haxby, 1978; McWilliams, 1987; May, 1994). While Probation is most discernible in its modern form from this period, in order to understand its originality fully, its history needs to be traced back to the period when the previous regime of order (feudalism) is dissolved and a new regime of subjugation is established in a form that is appropriate to the new society. That is, as part of the attempt to create a 'Society of Manners' that corresponded to the reconstituted political and civil society following the complete breakdown in law and order in the seventeenth century:

> Despite the fact that capital punishment was extending to include less serious infraction it proved to be an inadequate deterrent. Disorder was increasing. This led to calls for more terrible punishments including breaking offenders on the wheel, suspension on gibbets to die a long lingering deaths, branding, castrating and, in so far as women were concerned, indiscriminate transportation. But the fact that criminality was most prevalent in certain areas of the new metropolitan districts, concentrated attention on the manners and customs of the urban poor; leading to the connection between impropriety and immorality, drunkenness and depravity, lechery, prostitution, vagrancy, idleness.   (Radzinowicz, 1948/1956)

Laws already existed against immorality, although they were inadequately implemented and had fallen into disregard. It was now the primary object of the time to reassert them enthusiastically.

Immorality was not simply an individual problem, but was generalised into a major social issue. There was a connection between individual virtue and community security and property safety. The general problem of safety could be threatened by the sin of one person exciting God's anger against an entire population in the form of plagues; or individual depravity could threaten commercial life through, for example, decisions taken whilst drunk, which could lead to financial ruin affecting not just that particular sinner but the people with whom they traded. Profanity and debauchery were thus the worst enemies of the state. This link justified the practice of intervening in the life of the sinner:

> The grand seducer flatters men that he is freeing them from the bondage of religion, when he is enslaving them in the fetters of vice. The immoral man cannot be a good citizen, because he is not happy; and in his restlessness he imputes to the Government 'the distresses which flow from his own vices or impudence'.   (ibid.: 163)

'The Society of Manners' was established to eradicate this condition. It was formed out of the religious societies of the 1670s and 1680s in a context of the collapse of order inspired by immorality and corruption. The developed metropolitan society had a mission to (re)impose Christian private and public morality in the context of a tide of evil which appeared to have swamped London at this time. Appealing to a period of virtue after the Reformation and prior to the Restoration, the target for these societies were drunkenness, depravity and prostitution. Originating in East London, the society went on to establish a presence throughout the capital and eventually became a national movement.

The first society, set up in 1691, was composed of eminent lawyers, MPs, JPs and citizens of London of known ability and integrity. Most of the leaders of the societies came from 'the world of politics and business'. The movement spread quickly throughout the British isles. Widely supported by Church and state, it acquired added energy from 'The Society for Promoting Christian Knowledge', which was composed of senior members of the Church, whose specific aim was to reduce vice and immorality. Other societies were made up off lesser lights: tradesmen, or those taking part in parish administration, or constables able to discuss best practice and those capable of providing useful information.

INFORMING AND THE NEW SCIENCE OF INFORMATION

The effective instruments of intervention included aftercare and informal sanctions such as shaming and informing. Aftercare was the practice by which on release from county workhouses vagrants appeared before Quarter Sessions to be 'registered and recorded', so that upon re-offending they might more easily be convicted (Radzinowicz, 1948, Vol. 2). Informal sanctions were used to prevent criminality. These included public admonition, e.g. shaming through the production of public lists of offenders, and informing. Informing involved the collecting, processing and recording of information about individuals. Although despised, the information system formed the cornerstone of the Societies' activities. Through the processing of this information the societies supervised moral order in their localities. Through this process the society knew the detailed activity of all of the inhabitants in its jurisdiction and through this material could save individuals souls, avert the wrath of God and enforce the law (Curtis and Speck, 1976).

Informing was not the only focus for discontent. The religious zeal of the societies' members deviated into excess; and the concentration on the urban poor meant that very few of the rich were taken to task by these reforming zealots. Such was the extent to which their malpractices were enacted that Sydney Smith, writing at the time, felt that 'reformation generally produces greater evils than those it attempts to redress' (Radzinowicz, 1948: 179). Eventually, the societies degenerated into unpopular centres of sedition, dissent and sectarianism. By 1737 the 'Societies of Manners' had virtually ceased to exist, although rescued in different guises from time to time. By 1878 the societies had mutated into Voluntary Associations, for example, 'The Society for Giving Effect to his Majesty's Proclamation against Vice and Immorality' (1878) and 'The Society for the Suppression of Vice and Encouragement of Virtue' (1801).

EMBRYONIC

The genesis of the modern Probation Service can be discerned within this evangelical police force. G.D.H. Cole argues that these societies form the beginnings of the social services in the later centuries:

> They were probably the first voluntary groups organised on a national scale and tolerated by the government to step into a vacuum left by the inactivity of church and state and, in effect, to take over a part of the functions of the church and state and, therefore, despite their limitations must be considered an important part in the history of the creation of voluntary and free institutions.
>
>   (quoted in Bahlman, 1968: 107)

Whilst its form may be different from the 'Societies of Manners', many of the roles of the modern Probation Service remain remarkably similar to its original practice: admonition (shaming), intervening, aftercare and the role of information are all used today in Probation practice. And the problem of over-zealous practitioners was as much a problem in the eighteenth century as it was in the nineteenth and the twentieth centuries. But, be that as it may, the crucial point of this exposition of the genesis of the Probation Service is that the evangelical police reveal the origin not just of Probation, but of a moral order, at a time when it had not become naturalised or accepted as part of that order. That is a morality constructed on the intervention of money-capital, when whole new subjectivities were being invoked out of a post-revolutionary period.

MONEY, BIOGRAPHY AND VALUE – A THEORY OF ANTI-OPPRESSION

This anatomical investigation has demonstrated that (auto)-biographical life is a life lived as a human processed form of the social relations of capital. Money is the identity through which value expresses its personality: as oppressor (capital) and as oppressed (wage-labour). Each personality is the relation of value to itself. Each biography is the story of the (im)possibility of that relationship. Each personality is derived from characteristics of value in its oppressive (life-threatening) and anti-oppressive (life-giving) forms. Each biography is therefore unique and precisely the same. There is no humanity, there is only money and its identities. Liberal social science is a case of mistaken identity. What it imagines to be essential human characteristics are in fact characteristics of money-capital taken on and expressed in a human form.

This theory of anti-oppression points to the condition of cruelty rather than culture as the focus through which we should consider the human condition. In capitalist society the cruel power of money takes on the identity of *masculinity*. Masculinity is the expression of the cruelty, brutality and indifference of money-capital. In positions of power, women appear to take on the characteristics of men; in fact, they are taking on the identity of money. *Feminism* is the refusal of cruelty, an exposition of the brutal hierarchies of the power of money-capital dissolved through the flows of money as the satisfaction of human desire. In a world gone mad schizophrenia is the limit of the impossibility of human existence. More can be made of this: of course, *poverty* is the absence of money; *criminality* is the human condition of no money or a refusal to accept the law of money or the legal form of money: property rights; *class* is aggregated biography defined in relation to a life's position in the production of value and its realisation in exchange; currency is an important aspect of national identity; the struggle over a single European monetary system has as much to do with nationalism as it has to do with economics; social democracy is the avoidance of revolution through the redistribution of money; *Nazism* was the near-collapse of monetised society re-established as a Cruel State (Fascism); the *Jew*, in this condition, was the personification of the worst aspects of money-capital and held to atrocious account for the near-collapse of money society. The retribution of money-capital is terrifying.

To make these connections is not to suggest that the social enquiry is now at an end; but rather, to argue for the beginning of a real sociological enquiry. Money, on its own, changes nothing and explains nothing. And yet money is central to our understanding of the social world. From the biography of Moll Flanders, the aggregated biographies of Peter Linebaugh and from our own biographies, we know that it is possible for a life lived to demonstrate all or any or some characteristics of money-capital at any one time, or even at the same time. Each biographical or general life is lived in a particular way.

There can be, therefore, no one-dimensional theory of anti-oppression. An investigation into oppression demands an empirical investigation into each biography understood, not as a private life among other private lives, but as an institutionalised part of monetised society. There are no short-cuts; anything else is metaphysical speculation, or sheer intelligence. It is not enough for a theory of anti-oppression to explain that oppression to the oppressed. It must contain a manifesto for action. In the context of the Probation Service I make one claim: it is not offenders that must be rehabilitated, but money! Money can be rehabilitated when money-capital as exchange value (oppression) is subordinate to its other function, as use value (anti-oppression). That is, where the logic for the existence of money is not its own self-expansion but the logic of human need. In capitalist society this subordination is impossible. Rehabilitation demands the transformation of monetised society.

SHERBORNE HOUSE

In 1992 I was employed by the Inner London Probation Service as an Education Officer at Sherborne House, an alternative to prison project for young offenders in South London. Roger Graef, in *Living Dangerously* (1993), described Sherborne:

Operating from an old community building in South London, it is a showcase of the Inner London Probation Service. Many of the offenders who go there have already been to prison. They find Sherborne harder to take.

The building is on three storeys, with high ceilings, cold walls and cold floors. Sound bounces around the rooms making small groups seem like crowds. But it is free to the Inner London Probation Service, the gift of the Trustees of Sherborne School in the old tradition of helping the less fortunate. This is all the more telling as the bleak landscape of this part of South London is mocked by the opulence of the City just across the river. The staff augment their small budget with donated equipment that is all too scarce in other parts of the Probation Service... Staff have kitted out the art area with a darkroom and kiln. The music room has a range of synthesizers to create the current pop fashions. The tech workshop has a fine array of metal and wood-working gear. The work the young people have done there is astonishingly good.

They eat and play in 'the dining room' a large area that includes ping-pong and pool tables, as well as a makeshift kitchen and dining area.... the young cook, somehow produces the best institutional food I have ever eaten.... That the staff and offenders eat together seems normal in that atmosphere, but for it to happen in other penal establishments would take a radical change of attitude.

Behind the anonymous waiting area and the door with its passcode lies not only communal dining, but an ethical assault course. At the end of it is the chance for those who have come here to change their lives... (Graef, 1993: 7–8)

Twenty-four young offenders go through the ten-week programme (four programmes a year). Living at home or in hostels they attended the Centre every weekday from 9 am until 4 pm. Through concentrated group-work sessions the young offenders are forced to confront their lives as offenders through a process of shaming, by challenging their attitudes and moralities, by role-playing and by considering the position of the victim. These sessions are augmented by life-skills sessions and designated periods which deal with issues of racism and sexism. All these practices (or 'mind-games' as described by the young participants) are based on psychological theories of the cognitive nature of criminal activity and 'radical' criminological theories of discrimination. Time spent out of these intensive sessions includes creative practical activity in art, metal and wood-workshops, a music studio and on sporting and outdoor activities. Failure to attend or lateness are met with strict penalties which could result in the offender going to prison. Only half the original number starting the programme would ever complete. It was my job to assist the young offenders in the transition from the course back into mainstream education projects, training and work.

I did not come from the world of Probation. I had worked since 1978 on a range of programmes involved with young offenders and the young unemployed. I had been through all of the options, alternatives and ways of dealing with the problem. Nothing worked. And, what is more, the situation was getting worse for young people. In south-east London, education provision was shrinking, training schemes were universally despised, the employment market had collapsed and crime was escalating. The police had declared war on black youth, and the black youth were fighting back. The young people identified the problem themselves: 'The problem is money, money is everything.' All their crimes were to get money and they would do anything for money. Every youth at Sherborne said he would kill for money.

I called my part of the Sherborne experience 'The Futures' programme, with a subtitle 'the future is now'. We had just ten weeks, and we had to do something fast. For the youths on the programme there was no future. 'Now' was an imperative. I had money. A major supermarket chain gave the 'Futures' programme £24,000. I asked each youth in the group what he wanted to do, or to be. There was no limit, no refusals and nothing was considered to be unrealistic. Young people could get access to at least £500 from the

Futures Trust and were eligible for other monies from award-making bodies such as The Prince's Trust and London Youth Adventure. These organisations were extremely supportive and we used them extensively. The young people wanted to do everything. To go everywhere. To be someone. Money was not always the biggest problem. Foreign travel meant learning a language; being a rally driver meant learning how to drive and repair a car engine; learning to fly meant getting access to a plane; being a lawyer meant going to college. Each individual project was designed as an educational package. But it was only money that made it possible.

The 'Futures' programme was more than an educational part of the Sherborne programme. It did not challenge the offending behaviour of the young people; rather, it sought to challenge the intellectual basis of offending behaviour programmes at Sherborne and elsewhere in the Probation Service. Crime is not a just an ethical or moral or cultural or environmental or societal or economic or psychological or cognitive problem. It is all of these things, but they are only expressions of a more fundamental problem, i.e. a problem of real biography: the impossibility of social existence without money in a world where the social has been monetised. This intellectual challenge was not out of disrespect to any of my colleagues working in impossible circumstances; but rather, a practical critical project against the mainstream and radical ideologies within which they had been 'trained'.

What had been envisaged as an aspect of the programme began to take over the whole Sherborne timetable. The 'Futures' programme, for some young people, became the reason for being at Sherborne and for finishing the course, as the grant was awarded at the end of the programme. As the completion rates went up, young people who had previously refused and criticised other aspects of the programme were very positive about 'Futures'. It had other spin-offs. The purely educative aspect of my work, formerly an option for the young people, became compulsory at the suggestion of the young people themselves. They could work on their 'Futures' projects during these periods. Its success meant that it attracted interest from other programmes working with young people in the Inner London Probation Service. It became established in all teams in south London working with young people, including a women-only programme in north London, and it became an integral part of Temporary Prison Release Programmes.

While the Probation Service responded positively to the energy that the programme generated, despite the fact that the approach challenged the criminological assumptions upon which much of their reason for existing was based, the real tension between the different approaches was never far from the surface. The more ambitious the project became the more resentment was generated. This was not surprising. The logic of the 'Futures' programme did undermine the logic of the Probation Service. Colleagues demanded more control over how grants should be allocated. It had been left to me and the Senior Probation Officer to control the money, and more controls were demanded on how the young people dealt with the money. I wanted to give the money without any control, other than a request that receipts be provided and a commitment that the money be spent in the way in which it had been applied for. I said that any sanction would not be against the young people who had been awarded the money but youths coming after them, for whom it would not be possible to justify such a policy if it were abused. The money did get ripped off, but rarely; although each time it happened the pressure mounted against the scheme.

Generally, the programme was regarded as a success. Kenneth Clarke, then Home Secretary, visited the project and accepted the 'Futures' programme as a challenging intervention. The same could not be said of his successor, Michael Howard. Howard was well known for his right-wing credentials, but the Criminal Justice System had not yet felt the full force of his reactionary instincts. On a visit to Sherborne he was surprised that such a project should exist in a penal institution. Our conversation went beyond the usual pleasantries associated with such visits: we had a real discussion, but not an argument. However, the tone of the meeting and the visit to Sherborne, which had not been a great success, made some of my less enthusiastic colleagues anxious as to the appropriateness of the money-giving scheme. Their anxieties were heightened by the spate of tabloid newspaper stories featuring young offenders from other projects on safari holidays, paid for at taxpayers' expense and justified as remedial therapy. They feared, not unnaturally, for the reputation of Sherborne and their jobs.

Matters came to a head when weeks later an article appeared in the *Independent on Sunday*:

> When Michael Howard, the Home Secretary, visited the Sherborne House Probation Centre in Bermondsey, south London, in September he had his worst fears about liberal do-gooders confirmed. Staff [that's me] running Sherborne House, the community centre for juvenile offenders, proudly told him about an 18-year-old burglar who had learnt Spanish and would soon be heading to Madrid to test his skills. But far from being impressed the Home Secretary exploded. 'This is quite extraordinary!', he exclaimed, and began a hostile cross-examination to find out how it was that a young criminal could get a foreign holiday. Then Mr. Howard marched out. Decisive action followed. Last Wednesday David Maclean, the Home Office minister, told the Commons: 'Community penalties should be just that – penalties. A cushy foreign holiday . . . is clearly an unacceptable response to offending'. He promised new national standards which would ensure 'offenders receive proper punishment'. (*The Independent*, 5 December 1992)

This article, despite the fact it was an untrue and a sensationalist account of what had happened, generated a great deal of anxious interest. This anxiety and the resentment already felt, allied to the fact that colleagues with whom I had set up the project had now moved on, added to the fact that the 'Futures' approach had re-oriented the Sherborne approach to young offenders in ways that were unacceptable to the Probation staff working there, and, as a result, the project began to get severely squeezed. Management control was exerted more tightly. It became impossible to reconcile the demand created among the young people themselves with the logic of control demanded by Probation. I had begun to get closed down. I left Sherborne in 1994 aware that there were no plans to replace me and that the 'Futures' programme faced an uncertain future.

The programme had not solved anything, but it had focused on the problem as a problem of money-capital in a way that went against all prevailing criminological approaches. It treated money as a means of exchange, as a way of making the impossible possible and denied, for an instant, money as a supreme social power in a world where money is the supreme social power. For a brief moment in time money had been rehabilitated. Such an approach could not be allowed to continue.

5 LETS Abolish Money? Is there a Community Outside the Community of Money?

The past decade has seen the emergence and proliferation of local exchange and trading schemes (LETS) in the UK. Advocates have claimed that LETS constitute an important challenge to the global money economy. It is argued that LETS overcome the exploitation associated with the global money economy, that LETS overcome the fetishism of commodities inherent to the money economy and allow the unmediated production and exchange of use-values. In this way it is argued that LETS overcome the alienation inherent to the money form and allow for a revitalisation of local communities.

The small, self-sufficient communities envisaged by advocates of LETS is a well-established Utopia. There is an essential continuity between Adam Smith's tribe of hunters and shepherds trading sheep and vension and the postmodern eco-warriors trading New Age trinkets and alternative medicines. What these have in common is the way in which money is conceptualised. For both money is or can be simply a medium of exchange: a harmless device allowing the exchange of equivalent values between free and equal individuals. But whilst Adam Smith was concerned to overcome the simplistic formulation of the mercantilists, which suggested that profit derived from the accumulation of money, the postmodern eco-warrior blithely accepts the mercantilist proposition. They go on to repeat the nineteenth-century doctrines of Proudhon and his followers that the evils of capitalism can be avoided by robbing money of its status and privileges. Nowhere is this more obvious than in the claims being

91

made by 'green' commentators about the impact and possibilities of LETS.

These are bold claims and have been developed from theoretical perspectives which are explicitly anti-foundationalist
in their orientation: positions from which social forms such as
money are denied material determinations and historical context. In this chapter I subject these claims to the analytical
rigour of the historical materialist perspective and the analysis of money developed by Marx in both his early 'philosophical' writings and the later accounts developed in *Capital*
and the *Grundrisse*. I shall argue that Marx's approach is
highly relevant in analysing LETS for two main reasons.
First, Marx developed his own theory of money in the context of a monetary crisis and in opposition to writers such as
Proudhon, who believed that the contradictions of capitalism
could be overcome through the reform of the money system.
Second, a major preoccupation of Marx was the way in which
money destroyed communities and the way in which the
abstract regulation of society through money and the law
resulted in mystified and fetished struggles to reinvent communities on the basis of religion, nationality and locale. In
other words, Marx's approach allows us to explore both the
value relations underlying the development and operation of
LETS and the way in which LETS constitute a fetishised and
mystified reaction to the alienating contradictions of the
money-form.

LETS BEGIN WITH SOCIOLOGY...

Following the tenets of mainstream sociology it is possible to
analyse LETS as an ideology and as a social movement
emerging from the increasingly reflexive nature of the high-
or postmodern social order. In other words, we are back to
the cognitive and aesthetic models of social consciousness
derived from neo-Kantian and poststructuralist social
theory, which were analysed in chapter 3. As we saw earlier,
the category of *risk* has become a central motif in the models

of social action and consciousness derived from both positions. Whilst the academic literature on LETS is undeveloped, it is possible to construct models drawing on the dominant currents of (post)modern social theory. Developing the neo-Kantian approach, it is clear that money for writers such as Anthony Giddens (1990; see also Dodd, 1994) is a *symbolic token* universalised by the development of modernity as a means of linking 'economic' transactions in time and space. The development of LETS would reflect the increasing lack of *trust*, which reflexive individuals are prepared to invest in modern 'expert systems' such as the economy and the state, as modern 'symbolic tokens' are distorted by the increasingly intensive rate of development in the late-modern order. In this sense, it would be possible to conceptualise LETS as a form of local money created by reflexive individuals in an attempt to circumvent the risks of global money and foster increasing levels of trust among local networks of social actors. LETS could thus be seen as a 'utopian realist' strategy by a 'new social movement' premised on the *contextual* (re)negotiation of value and the circumvention of socially necessary labour-time by new negotiations of value on the basis of locally, and often interpersonally, constructed social relations (Lee, 1996). In other words, LETS is an attempt to reclaim the rationality of money which has been distorted by the increasingly out-of-control nature of the global money system.

The poststructuralist approach would presumably attempt to understand LETS as a counter-ideology: a discourse resistant to the totalising and globalising discourse of global money. The focus of LETS on the locale would be seen to highlight the way in which politics increasingly takes the form of a 'neo-tribalism' (Maffesoli, 1991), which rejects the abstraction inherent in the commodity and state forms for the immediacy of the locale and the personal relations contained therein (Lash and Urry, 1994). In this sense LETS would constitute a 'symbolic space' in which to recapture a sense of 'identity' and 'community' and to remoralise the spaces emptied out by the abstract dynamics of modernity.

LETS confront the dangers posed to the identity sustaining practices of the 'decentred' self: the risks posed to identity and affectation by the abstract circulation of images and symbols and a manifestation of cultural heterogeneity in the context of the homogenizing 'economic' dynamic of the global money system (Appadurai, 1990). In other words, LETS emerge in response to the increasingly totalising impact of money as an ideology or discourse.

The immediate problem with both the accounts anticipated above is the understanding of money on which they are premised. In one, money is merely a symbolic medium of exchange which has been de-rationalised by the distortions of high- or late modernity and can be re-rationalised through the semi-utopian reflexive projects of new social movements. In the other, money is merely a simulacrum: a totalising discourse detached from the 'real' economy which threatens totally to subsume the 'life-world' of individual social actors. I have thus returned in both accounts to the notion of money as 'sheer intelligence'. To return to Derrida (1992), the distinction between money as money and money as LETS is resolvable only in respect of the discursive meanings which are ascribed to these phenomena as forms of money. This, however, is highly problematic. Human subjectivity and consciousness cannot be constructed through money because in capitalist society money is the (partial) denial of subjectivity and consciousness. In capitalist society money articulates the historical form of alienated labour and is precipitated through an historical process which denies the integrity of human consciousness.

...SO LETS GET REAL!

In order to understand money we need to begin with an understanding of history and the relationship between history and human consciousness. In the process of history, individual wills are conditioned in 'class' ways; history is the result of contradictory class interests and forces and therefore human agency gives rise to involuntary results. There is a crucial ambivalence to our presence as human beings in history: 'part-subject, part-object, the involuntary agents of our own involuntary determinations' (Thompson, 1978: 88). In other words, individuals do not derive symbolic meanings from money and construct their subjectivity from cognitive or aesthetic structures of economic meaning. Money is a contradictory *social* form which both allows and denies human subjectivity. It is, therefore, important to analyse LETS in the context of the historical materiality of the crisis tendencies of capitalist development, as this allows for the development of LETS to be analysed as an important moment in the crisis and recomposition of the capital relation. This is important as Marx's theory of money was developed against the monetary crisis of 1857–8 (Bologna, 1993) and was premised on an attempt by Marx to highlight the way in which the crisis of money was merely the appearance of a more fundamental crisis of the capital relation. Marx used this critique to highlight the weakness of utopian socialist strategies which believed that the crises and contradictions could be overcome through the reform or abolition of money. Similarly, we can argue here that LETS have emerged in the context of a prolonged crisis of money (monetarism) and that LETS are a partial and mystified attempt to resist and refuse the money form.

LETS can become a genuine threat to the abstract power of money only if we really understand what money is and the role played by money in the social regulation of capitalism. This requires an engagement with the current sociological orthodoxy, which suggests that popular consciousness and political mobilisation are no longer informed by class, but by cultural characteristics and 'life-style'. The development of LETS is premised on an emergent 'green' ideology and membership of 'green' social movements is defined by a commitment to the ecological preservation of the planet and forms of 'alternative' lifestyles which support these objectives. In other words, new social movements constitute an idealist psychological reaction to the risks inherent to global modernisation, and, indeed, the academic literature on new social movements is dominated by accounts which focus on the psychological factors which result in the formation of ideological discourses (Beck, 1992, 1995; Giddens, 1990; Melucci, 1989; Tourraine, 1982). However, the ideologies of new social movements, and indeed all ideologies, are not fabrications or merely the projections of abstract ideas, but are the alienated forms of expression of historically developed social relations. An understanding of money and the social regulation of money is central to understanding the development and form of modern ideologies and the forms of consciousness and action articulated by new social movements.

In the *Communist Manifesto* Marx and Engels graphically describe the way in which feudal communities were 'pitilessly torn asunder' by the development of capitalist social relations and the way in which the 'nexus between man and man' had been reduced to naked self-interest and 'cash payment':

> Constant revolutionising of production, uninterrupted disturbance of all social conditions, everlasting uncertainty and agitation distinguish the bourgeois epoch from all earlier ones. All fixed, fast-frozen relations, with there train of ancient and venerable prejudices and opinions, are swept away, all new formed ones become antiquated before they can ossify. *All that is solid melts into air*, all that is holy is profaned, and man is at last compelled to face with sober senses his real conditions of life and his relations with his kind.   (Marx and Engels, 1965: 37; emphasis added)

Communities have been destroyed (dissolved into thin air) by the impact of money, and illusory communities have been constructed on the basis of the nation-state and religion. It is because money destroys community that the spiritual aspirations of individuals for a sense of moral community take on alienated forms such as religion and nationalism. In capitalist society the absence of a real community is thus compensated for through the construction of illusory communities of religion and the state. This illustrates the importance of placing the development of LETS in its historical context. Whilst the crisis of Keynesianism appears as a crisis of money (monetarism) it obscures a more fundamental crisis of the capital relation. The imagined communities and Utopias of Keynesianism (Fordism, social democracy, planning) have been destroyed by the global restructuring of capital. The discourse of the new social movements is an attempt to capture a new postmodern and neo-liberal form of 'associational' community. A community for the neo-liberal world based on flexible networks of associates. It constitutes an emergent 'do-it-yourself' culture emerging from a crisis of state planning and an increasing lack of trust in global money. The LETS networks epitomise neo-liberal forms of association.

While it is certainly the case that the politics of the new social movements could pose a threat to the new global order, this does not detract from the fetishised and alienated nature of 'community' underlying LETS ideology and practice. Below I explore this proposition further and argue that LETS constitute an *abstract* form of social regulation which perpetuates rather than ameliorates the fetishism of commodities, and that the struggle to restore humanity must be premised on the development of forms of social organisation and social consciousness through which humanity can bring its social powers under self-conscious control (Clarke, 1988). I shall begin by exploring the way in which LETS have developed in the UK and the social relations which are created and sustained by LETS networks.

WHAT ARE LETS?

There is nothing particularly new about local exchange and trading systems. The cooperative movement in nineteenth century Britain, various barter schemes which emerged in both the USA and Europe during the Great Depression of the 1930s, and the 'Time-Dollar' schemes which developed during the 1980s in the USA are all examples of locally-based schemes for fostering mutual cooperation and ameliorating the worst effects of the global money economy. There are,

however, a number of important ways in which LETS differ
from earlier schemes. First, LETS schemes are not based on
'barter' but allow exchange through a local 'currency'. Second, the LETS currency is not issued by a single body but is
created by the individuals who take part in the schemes.
There is thus no limit on the 'money supply'. Following
from these points LETS are presented as inherently empowering for the individuals taking part, allowing them to participate actively in the regeneration of their local economies.

The past decade has indeed seen a massive proliferation in
LETS. During the 1990s the number of LETS in the UK has
grown from five in early 1992 to 200 schemes with 20,000
members by late 1994 (Lang, 1994). These systems allow
individuals within a local community to exchange goods
and services outside the money economy. Goods and services
are traded through a unit of account which is given a name by
LETS members themselves and which is usually symbolically
related to the locale (New Berries in Newbury, Bobbins in
Manchester, Offas in Bishops Castle, Yorkies in York, etc.).
The members of the LETS scheme list the goods and services
they have to offer and the goods and services they desire in a
'directory', which also specifies the number of LETS units
charged for a particular service. The directory also gives the
telephone numbers of all members to the scheme in order that
individuals wanting to trade can contact each other directly,
agree a 'price' for the service and goods on offer, and carry
out the transaction. The transaction is 'paid' for through the
use of 'cheques' written out in the LETS unit, which are
subsequently sent to the treasurer of the association who
keeps records of all transactions and publishes regular state-
ments showing the balance for individual members.

In order to understand the way in which LETS work it is
important to explore the principles on which the schemes
were founded. The idea of LETS was first introduced into
the UK by Michael Linton, a Canadian, who set up a LETS
scheme in Courtenay, British Columbia, and who gave a
paper at a conference organised by 'new' or 'alternative'
economists to run alongside the G7 Economic Summit in

1986. According to Linton (1986), LETS are defined by five criteria:

1. LETS are non-profit making.
2. There is no compulsion to trade.
3. Information on balances is available to all members.
4. The LETS unit is equal in value to the national currency.
5. No interest is charged or paid.

The non-profit making status of LETS is essential in order that all spending reflects work done or services provided. This avoids the 'non-productive' trading in money which results from speculation and the charging of interest. LETS are thus premised on a particular view of what money is, and the role played by money in the social regulation of society. The view of money presented by leading advocates of LETS (see, for example, Lang, 1994) suggests that the essence of money is to provide a measure or record of the work carried out by individuals in order that they can be justly rewarded for their effort, skill and expertise. LETS are thus based on the 'new economics' philosophy, which regards alternative currencies as a way of encouraging the use of money as a means of exchange rather than a medium of exploitation (Sallnow, 1994). The problem of money, according to such a view, is that in the modern world money has become a commodity in itself and the speculative activities of banks and financial institutions, and the monetary policies of the state and supranational institutions, undermine the function of money as a measure of work; which instead becomes the means by which the state and transnational corporations dominate society. The main enemy is the 'interest' paid to speculators, which allows money to be earned without any work being done. The result is that huge sums of money constantly circulate the global financial systems, whilst there is simultaneously a shortage of money to pay workers to provide essential public needs.

The relationship between LETS and global currency can be broken down into four propositions or hypotheses, first outlined by Nader (1992). These propositions highlight the conceptualisation of money being developed by advocates of LETS:

1. The 'real' wealth of society derives not from money but from the *time* which people have to help others, and the willingness of people to use that time in helping others. LETS demonstrate that there is a substantial reservoir of time, which is untapped by the market economy.
2. Society has two economies: the market economy and the household economy of family neighbourhood and community. Many of the problems faced by society are a result of the erosion of the latter by the former.
3. Individuals respond to rewards other than money and society lacks the money to reward all the activity 'it' wants and needs. LETS respond to the fundamental human need to be needed and valued through a combination of additional purchasing power and psychological reinforcement.
4. Money – even a lot of it – cannot completely substitute for what the family, neighbourhood and the *community* used to provide.

There is a number of perceptive insights contained in the proposition, but there is also a number of limitations. The first two points correctly highlight the existence of time and space outside the global money system which could be used to fulfil human needs. There is, however, a failure to consider the differentiation between money-as-money and money-as-capital, and the way in which the latter involves the constant and increasing compression of time and space in response to the valorisation imperatives of the postmodern flexible accumulation strategy of global capital (Harvey, 1990). In other words, locating the time and space for initiatives such as LETS is likely to become increasingly less feasible the more intensified the process of global capital accumulation becomes.

Following from this the second two propositions are fundamentally flawed as they imply the voluntaristic generation of counter-cultures and counter-moralities 'outside' the economic dynamics of the global money system. They ignore the way in which postmodern morality (Bauman, 1991) and culture (Featherstone, 1991) are generated behind the backs of social actors through the material contradictions of post-modern capital accumulation (Jameson, 1991). There is a strong 'ethical' or 'moral' basis to LETS schemes which are articulated as an oppositional counter-culture against the fragmentation and alienation inherent to the abstract power of the global money system. This can be illustrated by exploring the principles of the LETS scheme in Brixton, south London, which is founded on the members' commitment to each other and the wider community and on the following ethical principles:

1. To foster trade within the local community in a cooperative spirit, particularly in those areas currently undervalued by the global money economy.
2. To empower every member of the community, particularly the unemployed and those working without pay, to take an equal role in its activities.
3. To encourage an awareness of the real value of goods and services – this involves minimising or excluding environmentally or socially damaging activities wherever possible.

LETS are thus presented as being a way of revitalising a sense of *community* and of redressing the problems created by the global money economy. LETS simultaneously provide an inflation- and risk-free currency whilst revitalising the social interconnectedness of individuals through a reconstruction of *community* and a rebuilding of trust. This is to be achieved through the re-moralisation of commodity-exchange in order to replace the *affective* content which has been emptied out by the abstract dynamics of the global money economy. As I shall show later in this chapter, this is highly problematic as money is the denial of affectivity. Affectivity implies a relationship charged with 'feeling', 'emotion' and 'desire'. In any society regulated through exchange-value, individuals only have relationships with *things*: a perverted and fetishised affectivity. The love of the thing denies the mutual and reciprocal love of others. The negation of real community is inherent in the money form. The problems of money cannot be overcome through the reform and re-moralisation of monetary relations because money denies the pre-existence of a moral or affective community outside the community of money.

LETS TRANSFORM SOCIETY?

Advocates of LETS argue that the schemes revitalise the sense of community within localities. Money is seen as resulting in the fragmentation of communities as the activities of transnational corporations physically destroy communities in order to seek out cheap labour in the global marketplace, whilst the anonymity of monetary transactions dissolves the 'affective' content of economic exchange. LETS, it is argued, overcome the anonymous and abstract relationships which have resulted from the dominance of the money economy. The schemes break down barriers of social class and cultural difference and allow members to make friends with people from a diverse range of social backgrounds. LETS constitute, therefore, an attempt to revive a sense of 'community' (*neo-Gemeinschaften*) within the locale. Following the edicts of communitarian philosophy (for example, MacIntyre, 1981, 1988; Taylor, 1989; Walzer, 1983), LETS allow the 'democratisation' and 'reflexive mediation' of money as an 'expert system' and provide a solidaristic basis for the creation of 'green' micro-communities. LETS are presented as a way by which local communities can wrest an element of local control back from the nation-state and the global economy. LETS are thus an important moment in an emergent 'green' discourse, and the circumvention of money is usually linked to the environmental costs imposed by the operation of the global money economy. The forces of competition result in a global division of labour and the movement of goods and labour around the globe in ways which threaten to destroy the natural environment. LETS schemes are thus also said to have important ecological benefits as the production and exchange of local services avoid the need to transport goods over large distances and therefore reduce pollution in the form of CO^2 and packaging. LETS allow a more efficient use of non-renewable resources through the way they encourage the sharing of expensive equipment and the repair rather than the replacement of defective consumer durables.

LETS have also been presented as a way of countering the problem of long-term unemployment. In the context of the present crisis, it allows cash-starved communities to release the skills and competencies of individuals and thereby enrich the local community. LETS schemes have the potential to widen the contacts and skills of the long-term unemployed and provide them with access to expensive capital equipment which would be needed in order for them to set up in business. LETS allow for the re-vitalisation of local communities through the way in which the wealth created through the schemes does not leak out of the locale through the profits and interest paid to TNCs and banks, and encourages individuals to use local services rather than imports from across the globe. In this sense LETS are indeed a way of avoiding the risks inherent in the global money system. As a leading member of the Haverfordwest LETS group argued:

> If you give me a cheque for 50 'lets' it could not possibly bounce. No one loses anything by the deficit incurred. Its your deficit that's all. There's no interest charged, no fixed time to pay, the liability just sits there in a book or a computer. LETS can't be stolen or borrowed: you can't use them outside your area, so there is an inbuilt *trust*.
>
> (*Guardian*, 12 March 1994)

In a study of a LETS scheme in Calderdale, Williams (1996) found that whilst the scheme did bring important benefits to the poor and unemployed workers, the operation of the scheme reproduced the advantages and disadvantages of the money economy. This was particularly the case in respect of the *price* paid for the goods and services provided by professional and middle-class members of the scheme. Indeed, LETS schemes are currently clustered in affluent areas with low unemployment, and there is evidence of the (unintentional) exclusion of marginalised individuals on the grounds of 'taste' or 'life-style'. In other words, the access to LETS schemes is regulated by what participants have to *offer* rather than what other members can *give*. As we shall see, this is a result of the existence of LETS communities within the wider community of money. The abstract nature of regulation, and the technical and educational resources required to run a LETS scheme, serves to exclude marginal social groups and, as a result, LETS schemes are dominated by professional and educated elites.

There is also the extent to which LETS are ideologically dominated by 'green' ideologies through the well-developed links between green activists in both local schemes and the national LETS Development Agency. In this sense Lee (1996) argues that LETS are socially and ideologically dominated by an emergent graduate underclass: a lumpen-intelligentsia made up of green, vegetarian but unemployed graduates. In this sense LETS schemes often exclude the poor on the grounds of 'taste' and 'life-style'. This has often been partially overcome by the involvement of local authorities (i.e. the state) in the establishment of LETS schemes. This is reflected in the geographical concentration of LETS schemes in the UK, which as Lee demonstrates, are in relatively affluent areas. Lee argues, therefore, that LETS are part of an attempt to develop a locally defined 'moral economy': an attempt to resist the power of money to 'disinfest' the moral content from economic transactions; an attempt by local people to restore a moral content to transactions through direct social relations and trust. The legitimacy of the LETS schemes is thus based on trust and reciprocation. This is one of the most potent sources of exclusion in the operation of LETS schemes: the basis of trust in a society dominated by private property is mistrust and only the trustworthy are given access to the community.

LETS TRANSFORM CAPITALISM?

LETS attempt to confront one of the principal contradictions of capital accumulation: that human needs and capacities are subordinated to the valorisation of capital. Capital accumulation is marked by the coexistence of two simultaneously occurring circuits of money and commodities: M-C-M' and C-M-C. Needs and capacities which cannot be subordinated to the circuit M-C-M' are not met or utilised. LETS are presented as a way of circumventing the circuit M-C-M' by allowing the local mediation of needs and capacities through a circuit C-M-C. LETS thus allow trading to take place where money in the form of sterling is not available through the way in which they create interest-free credit on demand for members of the schemes. LETS are presented as a powerful mechanism for regenerating the local economy. The wealth created in the form of LETS currency is specific to the locality and the non-transferability of LETS currency means that locally produced wealth is reinvested locally for the benefit of the community. The unemployed, for example, can trade in LETS schemes and acquire skills and resources without the need for 'credit', which would inhibit their escape from poverty in the money economy. This is because LETS schemes allow members to spend before they have earned. Members who spend are not seen as being 'in debt' but being 'in commitment' to the community to do work in the future. In this sense, creating LETS units by spending is seen as a 'social service' as it allows others to spend and thereby enriches the wealth of the community. The publication of accounts allows for the regulation of the system to be based on mutual and informal recognition of positive and negative balances by members of the scheme. Members with high negative balances are approached with offers for them to offer work/services, whilst members with high positive balances are approached by individuals keen to sell to them.

As mentioned earlier, prominent advocates of LETS argue that the LETS currency should be roughly equivalent to sterling. In the UK 65 per cent of LETS schemes currently link their LETS unit to sterling (Lang, 1994: 150). For many advocates of LETS the importance of relating the LETS currency to the national currency is important in order to attract small local businesses to participate in the schemes. Small businesses will often charge for goods in proportions of LETS currency and sterling depending on cash-flow requirements. Local businesses are able to benefit from the schemes owing to the way in which their customer base is expanded by people who are LETS-rich but cash-poor. Local businesses also benefit from LETS schemes through the way in which they enable extra workers to be paid or part-paid in LETS. Whilst most LETS schemes do relate the value of the LETS unit to sterling, a further ethical element of the schemes is that individuals participating in the schemes are able to 'revalue' work according to the individual circumstances of the traders. Rather than the anonymous and abstract relationships which mark the money economy, the individuals participating in LETS schemes are often personally known to each other and can account for one of the parties being unemployed or disabled. Furthermore, work given a low value in the money economy, but which is tedious, arduous or dirty, can be revalued to reflect the socially useful nature of dirty but essential jobs. For this reason, LETS are also presented as having positive implications for gender relations as they allow a revaluation of the jobs and services traditionally provided by women. These concerns have led other LETS schemes to reject the idea that the LETS currency should be tied to sterling and have either made the LETS unit time-based or have introduced time-based factors into the way in which the value of goods and services are calculated.

LETS clearly offer an opportunity for the unemployed to attain useful work and for individuals to gain access to useful goods and services when they do not have the money to pay for them. It has been claimed that the operation of LETS implies a form of regulation which undermines the fetishism of commodities (Lee, 1996). In a LETS system, it is argued, the money supply is not controlled by a central bank but by the requirements of exchange. Needs and indebtedness drive the system, and equilibrium is achieved through public accountability achieved through the publication of members' balances. Members of LETS schemes are, moreover, involved in direct, face-to-face contact with the individuals with whom they are trading and, therefore, allow individuals to develop an understanding of economy based on immediate and observable cause and effect. This is a highly problematical argument and demonstrates a lack of understanding in respect of the way in which capitalism works.

LETS are based on the immediate satisfaction of wants and needs and there is no potential within LETS for the production of a social surplus in order to support expanded reproduction (Lee, 1996). LETS are thus structurally tied to a wider, surplus-generating system as there is no surplus generated which can be devoted to expanded reproduction. What are these structural and institutional linkages? Whilst the businesses involved in LETS schemes are able to ease cash-flow and liquidity problems through the expansion of local markets, the implications for labour may be far less beneficial. The commodification and monetisation of society increases the dependence of individuals on the money-form through the way in which time and money become increasingly interlinked. In the context of the mechanisation of low-skilled labour-intensive work, alongside the commodification of leisure, LETS may thus serve further to exclude individuals on the margins of society (Offe and Heinze, 1992). Why do LETS appear to reproduce the alienation and inequality inherent in the capitalist system with which it forms a social totality? It should be immediately apparent that LETS do not aim to abolish money but to 'remoralise' the content of monetary transactions. As one of the leading national co-ordinators of the LETS network commented:

> The Thatcher years have really taken the humanity out of doing business. So much trading is depersonalized now. You go to the shops and don't talk to anyone. This way you are directly trading your skills and goods, you are individually creating a currency.   (*Guardian*, 12 March 1994)

The morality is premised on the morality of market exchange: of equal commodity-owners meeting in the moral market and engaging in the exchange of equivalents. Socially necessary labour-time is not abolished, but rather, becomes the touchstone for communitarian integration. The involvement of the local state in LETS mirrors the role of the law in the social regulation of capitalism, maintaining the illusion of equality in the sphere of exchange in order to obscure the inequalities and domination of labour in the sphere of production (Holloway and Picciotto, 1991). In order to understand this point, we need to delve beneath the surface of the money form and explore the value relations underlying the articulation of LETS as a social form.

VALUE RELATIONS WITHIN THE LETS NETWORK

The methodological approach developed by Marx in *Capital* can be developed in order to analyse the value relations underlying LETS. The approach was outlined by Marx in the 'Introduction' to the *Grundrisse* in which Marx argued that in order to understand the social relations underlying the fetishised categories of bourgeois society it was necessary to start from the simplest and most abstract determination and to proceed from these simple (abstract) determinations to the analysis of more complex (concrete) forms as a 'rich aggregate of many determinations and relations' (Marx, 1973: 101).

In capitalist society the simplest social form in which the products of labour are recognised is the commodity. Labour takes the form of and is socially realised through the commodity. The commodity is a contradictory social form owing to the way it articulates the contradiction between use-value and exchange-value: that concrete and useful labour is mediated by and only becomes socially realisable through its opposite – *abstract labour*. The contradictory determination of the commodity determines the alienation of human needs. Needs are met only if there is an effective demand for

them in the market (Heller, 1974). The social relations underlying LETS do not diverge from this basic form: LETS exchange taking the form C-M-C (or commodity-LETS unit-
commodity). The argument is, however, that whilst LETS
exchange may consist of the exchange of commodities it
avoids the alienation inherent to the fetishism of commodities. In capitalist society this alienation occurs because social
relations between people takes the form of the fetishised
relations between things: commodity production results in the
'illusion' by which things are ascribed characteristics originating in the social relations between men. The way in which:

> Social relations inevitably took the form of things and could
> not be expressed except through things. The structure of the
> commodity economy causes things to play a particular and
> highly important social role and thus acquire particular
> social properties.   (Rubin, 1972: 5)

Things come to play a social role owing to the distinctive
character of the commodity economy. The management and
organisation of production is constituted by independent
commodity producers who produce for society rather than
for themselves. The universal alienation of the products of
these independent producers through exchange or the market
results in the development of a unified productive system: the
distinctive feature of this system being the way in which the
market regulates the production of use-values or things. In
the commodity economy, commodities (indirectly) regulate
the working activity of people as the direct production of
use-values must take into account the expected conditions
of the market. The conditions of capitalist reproduction,
therefore, define the social character of labour. The working
activity of one member of society is affected by the work
activity of others only through *things*. Social relations inevitably take on a reified form: the form in which they both
exist and are realised. The 'thing' is an intermediary of
social relations, and the circulation of things both expresses
and creates production relations among men (Rubin, 1972:
7–13).

We need to assess, therefore, the extent to which production and consumption through LETS escapes the fetishism of commodities. It remains the case that individuals within LETS networks are unable to fulfil their own needs and capacities except through the objectification of their labour on the market. They have to offer some *thing* which is desired by another commodity owner in order to realise the *value* of their own commodity. In other words, the social relations underlying LETS is that of exchange-value. Exchange-value emerges as the regulatory form of a commodity producing society through a real process of abstraction. This emerges from the contradictory determination of the commodity: the contradiction between use-value and exchange-value. The labour contained in use-values is of a particular useful and concrete kind, but as exchange-values, determined by labour-time, the qualitative difference between use-values must be eliminated, and the labour that creates exchange-value is constituted by abstract, homogeneous, general labour. The labour contained in exchange-value is specifically social labour – labour for itself: abstract labour – labour that is constantly determined as 'human labour in general' or 'simple' labour by a real social process of abstraction.

In a society of generalised commodity production the production of use-values, the social division of concrete, useful labour, is regulated by the law of value. To what extent, then, do LETS escape the law of value? Individuals within LETS networks produce for exchange rather than to satisfy their own needs directly. In such a case the LETS unit is not a direct embodiment of concrete, useful labour, but it exists as a social form that has been created through a real process of abstraction and thus represents abstract social labour: labour abstracted from the particular use-value through which it was created. The relationship between LETS and the national currency also suggests that LETS production does not entirely escape the abstract dynamic of socially necessary labour time. LETS units are either directly related to the national currency or directly represent the labour-time attributed to the commodity. Either way, commodities can be exchanged only if they produce universal equivalents.

Hence, I have established that the production and exchange of commodities through LETS is a contradictory social process owing to the contradiction between use-value and exchange-value that is inherent the commodity. But capitalism is not simply based on the production and exchange of commodities. Capitalism is a particular form of generalised commodity production premised on the self-expansion of value. LETS is premised on the exchange of equivalents through the circuit C-M-C. The valorisation of capital is premised on the self-expansion of value in the circuit M-C-M'. Clearly, money has a different form and function in these two circuits. In the circuit C-M-C money is a means of exchange and circulation. In the circuit M-C-M' money is the most abstract manifestation of capital. The important point is that money is merely one of the forms in which capital exists. It is, moreover, a form which obscures the inequality and domination of living labour within the capital relation. We are thus left with two problems. First, LETS do not overcome the alienation inherent to the money form. As we shall see in the next section it is impossible to develop community and friendship through money because money is the denial and negation of community and friendship. Second, money exists in many forms and it is important to analyse LETS in the context of all these forms. When LETS are analysed in the context of money as capital, what is evident is that advocates of LETS have greatly overemphasised both the extent to which LETS challenge the global money system and the potential of LETS to overcome the problems of this system.

LETS BE FRIENDS! MONEY, LOVE AND FRIENDSHIP

LETS do not escape the contradictions and alienation inherent in the commodity form. This would seem to render prob-

lematic one of the central propositions of the LETS philosophy: that LETS strengthen the interpersonal bond between
individuals allowing people to forge friendships and mutual
respect amongst the individuals with whom they exchange
commodities. I shall explore this through the following hypo-
thetical proposition:

> I want to explore how I can affirm both my individuality
> and self-worth and my connectedness and friendship (love)
> with my fellow LETS-wielding communitarians. I live in
> south west England, a prosperous region integrated into
> the global money system through the manufacture and
> servicing of weapons of mass destruction. I am an electri-
> cian and have a useful service (commodity) to offer my
> fellow scheme members and have time to spare in between
> my self-employed contracts in the defence industry. There
> are, in the town in which I live, pockets of poverty caused
> by the decline of manufacturing and the capitalization of
> agriculture. By joining the LETS scheme I can offer useful
> services which fulfil other people's needs whilst simultane-
> ously helping others to escape poverty and thereby help to
> restore a sense of integration and community. I can also
> help myself to maximize the commodities that I am able to
> produce and exchange. So what kind of community is this?
> What kind of friendship (love) am I extending to my fellow
> man.

In order to approach the above proposition we need to
begin by recognising that LETS exchange is premised on the
commodity and that the *real* value of the commodity lies in
exchange-value. In other words, the commodities that I produce and consume through the LETS is mediated by
exchange-value. Thus the relationship with fellow LETS
members is mediated by a 'thing'; a thing which transforms
me from a real, living individual into an abstract caricature of
myself. LETS are currencies based on exchange-value and
mediate the relationship between members of a scheme. If I
alienate this mediating function, I remain active only as a
lost, dehumanised creature:

Through this *alien mediator* man gazes at his will, his activity, his relation to others as a power independent of them and of himself – instead of man himself being the mediator for man.... It is obvious that this *mediator* must be a *veritable God* since the mediator is the real power over that with which he mediates me.... Hence this *mediator* is the lost, estranged *essence* of private property, private property *alienated* and external to itself; it is the *alienated mediation* of human production with human production, the *alienated* species activity of man.... Thus man separated from this mediator becomes poorer as the mediator becomes richer.

(Marx, 1975a: 260–1; emphasis in the original)

Thus, when I am engaged in exchange I am not engaged in a human relationship, but am engaged in an abstract relationship of private property with private property. Even with LETS, money exists as the *abstract* form of private property and, consequently, money is the *true* value of things and the most desirable thing of all. Value can only be expressed through the LETS unit and, therefore, value exists only as money and money robs me of my humanity. The morality of LETS does not extend beyond the morality of money.

This abolition of estrangement, this return of man to himself and thus to other men, is only an *illusion*. It is a *self-estrangement*, dehumanization, all the more *infamous* and *extreme* because its element is no longer a commodity, metal or paper, but the *moral* existence, the *social* existence, the very heart of man, and because under the appearance of mutual *trust* between men it is really the greatest *distrust* and a total estrangement.

(Marx, 1975a: 263; emphasis in the original)

Money is perfected through abstraction: the more abstract money is, or the less natural (i.e. organically related) to the commodities mediated by money, the more perfect money becomes. LETS create pure money: money as pure unmediated credit. Whilst interest is not paid on LETS credit, the social relations underlying LETS are nevertheless determined by credit relations. LETS are premised on the creation of free credit and based on trust. But the content of trust is *money*. Through credit I transform myself into money and I meet the lender/borrower as money. The only *recognition* between us is the money advanced through credit. As Marx (ibid.: 264) notes, credit is only extended in two situations:

1. A rich man extends credit to a poor man whom he regards as industrious and orderly.
2. Credit facilitates exchange, i.e. it is money raised to a completely ideal (pure) form.

Credit is thus an economic judgement on the morality of man and therefore deeply immoral. It constitutes the evaluation of human life through money. Credit will only be extended to an individual considered worthy of credit. With private property the only morality is the morality of money.

In the credit system *man* replaces metal or paper as the mediator of exchange. However, he does this not as a man but as the *incarnation of capital and interest.* . . . Man is himself transformed into money, money is *incarnate*. Human individuality, human *morality*, have become both articles of commerce and the *material* which money inhabits. The substance, the body clothing the *spirit of money* is not money, paper, but instead it is my personal existence, my flesh and blood, my social worth and status. Credit no longer actualizes money-values in actual money but in human flesh and human hearts.

(Marx, 1975a: 264; emphasis in the original)

Credit reduces my worth to my worth as defined by money. Credit demoralises the poor as they suffer the ignominy and humiliation of having to ask the rich for credit. Moreover, the credit relationship implies that the counterfeiting of money must be carried out on man himself rather than on some other material. The credit relationship is thus defined by deception and exploitation: the basis of trust is mistrust –

mutual mistrust and, therefore, hate (not-love). The estrangement of man through money is simultaneously the denial of
true human *community*. A true community cannot emerge
when individuals recognise each other only as abstract in-
carnations of money. Community requires man to recognise
herself as man with needs and capacities mediated through
self-activity rather than the thing (money). The community of
LETS is not an authentic community as recognition is based
on the production and consumption of LETS currency units.
LETS and the proponents of LETS thus naturalise and take
for granted a notion of civil society based on a community of
private property owners. LETS traders face each other in a
relation of *mutual alienation*: an alienation which denies the
possibility of real community and which reinforces the divi-
sions inherent to the abstract regulation of society through
exchange-value:

> The reciprocal complementing and exchange of human
> activity itself appears in the form of: the *division of labour*.
> This makes man, as far as is possible, an abstract being, a
> lathe, etc., and transforms him into a spiritual and physical
> abortion. The very unity of human labour is regarded only
> in terms of division because man's social nature is realized
> only in its antithesis, as estrangement.
>
> (Marx, 1975a: 269; emphasis in the original)

The essence of exchange-value is indifference (brutality).
The equivalence between commodities takes on an independent form as *money*. Money is the unfettered domination of
the thing over man: the power of the product over the producer. LETS do not overcome this alienation. As in all production based on private property, man produces only in
order to *have* – having is the aim of production and therefore
has a *selfish* aim. The only reason that I make my abilities as
an electrician available within the LETS community is so that
I can *have* the French cottage that belongs to someone else for
my summer vacation. My relationship with others remains a
relationship mediated by *things*: correctly wired electrical
sockets for a pile of stone and timber in Provence:

I have produced for myself and not for you, just as you
have produced for yourself and not for me.... Each of us
sees in his product only his *own* objectified self-interest,
hence in the product of others the objectification of a
different, alien self-interest, independent of oneself.

(ibid.: 274–5; emphasis in the original)

Behind the appearance of mutual supplementation is
mutual plundering and deception. This is necessarily the
case in a social configuration based on self-interest (self-
love): mutuality based on a struggle for superiority. The
value which emerges from this mutuality is nothing but the
value of our mutual objects: I myself am worthless. LETS do
not constitute the unmediated satisfaction of human needs
and, therefore, deny both my individuality as a man and my
love and affirmation of you:

I would have acted for you as the *mediator* between you
and the species, thus I would be acknowledged by you as
the complement of your own being, as an essential part of
yourself. I would thus know myself to be confirmed both in
your thoughts and your *love*.

(ibid.: 277; emphasis in the original)

In any system of private property labour is not-life: it is the
alienation of life – *living death*. Whilst it appears as if individuality is confirmed through private property, it is in fact
the denial of true individuality and true community. The
affective content of LETS is thus the alienated and fetishised
self-interest of a micro-community of petty commodity producers. You are my friend and I love you because of what
you *have* rather than what I can *give* to you. I will not offer
my services as an electrician unless I know that I am going to
receive something in return. LETS confirm, therefore, the
alienation inherent in private property. LETS exist, moreover, in a social totality marked by a particular kind of
private property – the generalisation of wage-labour and the
command of living labour-power by dead labour – capital
(ism).

LETS ABOLISH MONEY? THE RETURN OF THE 'TIME-CHITTERS'!

The theory of money presented by advocates of LETS is not new, but was propounded in detail by the French utopian socialist Pierre Proudhon and his followers, such as Alfred Darimon, in the nineteenth century. The critique of Proudhon was a critical moment in the development of Marx's *Capital* (Rosdolsky, 1977: 99). Like his latterday counterparts, for Proudhon, the principal evil of the capitalist order was the privilege of money and the exploitation of labour in the sphere of exchange through the practice of usury. Proudhon argued that the exploitation of labour, and the resulting economic crises, could be resolved by robbing money of its privileges and making all commodities directly exchangeable. The LETS schemes are not directly the same as the schemes advocated by Proudhon, as many of the former schemes reject a time-based formulation in respect of the value of the LETS unit. What they share, however, is a concern to rob money of its privileges and to reduce money to the level of the rabble.

In the *Grundrisse* Marx undertook a detailed critique of Proudhon and his schemes for abolishing money. Proudhon recognised that in a society with a developed and systematic division of labour, direct barter was impracticable, and that a symbol or token was required in order to facilitate the reciprocal exchange of commodities. Proudhon argued that the value of labour could be represented by paper chits and that this would allow workers themselves to benefit from the increasing efficiency of living labour-power through the constant appreciation of the currency. The advocates of LETS repeat the mistakes of Proudhon in the way in which value and price are conflated and the way in which the necessary antagonism between these two forms is ignored. This distinction was outlined by Marx in the *Grundrisse*:

> The *value* (real exchange-value) of all commodities (labour included) is determined by their cost of production, in

other words, by the labour time required to produce them. Their *price* is this exchange-value of theirs expressed in money. The replacement of metal money (or of paper or fiat money denominated in metal money) denominated in labour-time would therefore equate the *real value* (exchange value) with their *nominal value, of value and price.*

(Marx, 1973: 136–7; emphasis in the original)

As Marx goes on to argue, the value of commodities as determined by labour-time is only their *average* value. Whilst the average value appears as an abstraction, it is a *real* abstraction owing to the way in which it exists as the 'driving force' and the 'moving principle' of the oscillations through which commodity prices run in a given period of time. Market value equates itself with real value through a constant non-equation with itself (as the negation of the negation: as the negation of itself as negation of real value). Price is distinguished from value not only as the nominal from the real, but because the latter appears as the law of motion through which the former runs. This has important implications in respect of the time-chits proposed by Proudhon:

The time-chit representing *average labour time* would never correspond to or be convertible into *actual labour time* i.e. the amount of labour-time objectified into a commodity would never command a quantity of labour-time equal to itself . . . just as at present every oscillation of market values expresses itself in a rise or fall of the gold or silver prices of commodities.   (ibid.: 139)

The time-chit would thus represent an 'ideal' labour-time which would oscillate above or below the real labour-time. This ideal labour-time would, therefore, become reified and achieve a separate existence of its own within which the time-chit would correspond to the non-equivalence. The result would be *alienation* because with the time-chit – as with any kind of money – 'the exchange relation establishes itself as a power external to and independent of the producers' (ibid.: 146). Money is both the form and content of general wealth and confronts individual commodities as an alien 'thing' with its own laws, equipped with all the properties which money has at present but unable to perform the same services. The circulation of commodities and the non-equivalence of value and price result in the emergence of money as a separate mode of existence. In this sense the time-chit cannot act as money because:

> Price is not equal to value, therefore the value-determining element – labour-time – cannot be the element in which prices are expressed, because labour-time would then have to express itself simultaneously as the determining and the non-determining element, as the equivalent and non-equivalent of itself.   (ibid.: 140)

Proudhon, therefore, made the mistake of equating value and price, and this enabled him to imagine that he had demolished the real differences and contradictions between the two forms. He could then imagine that he had further resolved all the contradictions of capitalism: the money price of the commodity equals the real value; demand equals supply; production equals consumption; money is simultaneously abolished and preserved; and the labour-time embodied in the commodity is directly embodied in the time-chit (Rosdolsky, 1977: 104). In this way all commodities are transformed into money; or, as Marx prosaically put it, 'let the pope remain but make everybody pope' (Marx, 1973: 138).

The fundamental weakness of Proudhon, according to Marx, was his failure to recognise the intimate relationship between commodities and money: the way in which the circulation of commodities inevitably gives rise to the emergence of money, and the impossibility of abolishing money while exchange-value remained the social form of products. These criticism led Marx to pose a question which has direct relevance in respect of LETS schemes:

> Can the existing relations of production and the relations of distribution which correspond to them be revolutionized by a change in the instrument of circulation, in the

organization of circulation?...Can such a transformation of circulation be undertaken without touching the existing relations of production and the social relations which rest on them?   (ibid.: 122)

Clearly, for Marx the social form of circulation rests upon a particular social form of production, and that changes in the form of circulation presuppose a change in the social form of production. The equivalence effected by money is above all the equivalence of social inequality: 'money hides a content which is eminently a content of inequality, a content of exploitation, the relation of exploitation is the content of the monetary equivalent' (Negri, 1991: 26). The tinkering with the instruments of circulation through LETS, therefore, constitutes an attempt to remoralise the demoralised community of money. Money is a relation of inequality: a generic representative of the property relation:

> The reciprocal and all-sided dependence of individuals who are indifferent to one another forms their social connection.... The power which each individual exercises over the activities of others or over social wealth exists in him as the owner of *exchange values*, of *money*. The individual carries his social power, as well as his bond with society, in his pocket.   (Marx, 1973: 157; emphasis in the original)

The usefulness of Marx's account of money in the *Grundrisse* is that it presents money in the form of a social relation and illustrates the way money represents, organises and sanctions these relations. Marx presents the real world as a world made of money with class struggle constituted by the denunciation and the refusal of money (Negri, 1991: 21–40). It also allows us to assess the claims of the communitarians: that LETS is an example of the way in which the globalising tendencies of (post)modernity open up spaces for the revitalisation of local communities. As Marx noted:

> Monetary greed, or mania for wealth, necessarily brings with it the decline and fall of the ancient communities (*gemeinwesen*). Hence it is the antithesis of them. (Money)

is itself the community (*gemeinwesen*) and can tolerate none
other standing above it.   (Marx, 1973: 223)

In a society dominated by exchange-value money is the
community: there is no community outside the community
of money. In a society dominated by exchange-value the
community is a reification. The form is *the* contradiction: it
is the antagonism which the circulation of money attempts to
terminate and resolve. Money does not create the contradictions of capital accumulation, rather it is the development
of the contradictions and antitheses which create the seem-
ingly transcendental power of money (Marx, 1973: 146). The
problem with Proudhon – and this can be directly levelled
against the advocates of LETS – is that his is an attempt to
resolve the antagonism within the sphere of circulation, and
thereby, further to mystify the exploitation inherent in
the money form. The reform of money, particularly the
socialisation of money by the state, is thus a deepening of
exploitation.

LETS SOLVE THE CRISIS?

It is impossible for LETS to overcome the crisis and contradictions of money. The advocates of LETS repeat the mistakes of Proudhon in failing to differentiate between money
as a means of circulation and money as capital. This is very
important if we are to understand the origins of the current
crisis of money (monetarism) and the extent to which initiatives such as LETS are able to provide a challenge/solution to
the present crisis. The provision of free credit (as through
LETS) would not overcome the crisis as a lack of money is
not at the origin of capitalist crisis. In a crisis, commodities
(including in particular the labour commodity) remain
unsold, *not* because there is a lack or absence of money but
because there is nothing against which they can be exchanged.
In other words, the contradictions of money derive *not*
from the form or the existence of money but from the social

relations of production mediated by money. In capitalist society, production is related to the generation of surplus-value rather than to meeting human needs, and there is thus no reason why supply and demand should balance. The lack of demand *appears* as a shortage of money and confronts producers as the power of money. The contradiction is not, however, created by money: rather, it is the contradiction between use-value and exchange-value that creates the power of money.

So what of the moralisation and democratisation of money advocated by the LETS-wielding modern-day time-chitters? In the context of a prolonged crisis of social capital (Keynesianism), and the recomposition of social capital (monetarism), LETS schemes ameliorate the monetary appearance of the crisis: i.e. no money (as poverty, unemployment, crime, demoralisation). The poverty and demoralisation which appear as an absence of money obscures the content of the crisis – as a crisis and struggle over the extraction of surplus-labour and the realisation of surplus-value. The antagonistic foundations on which money is premised allow money to emerge as a 'social symbol' and as a 'function of command': the 'money subject' determined as both a consequence of the crisis and as a solution. The dialectic is not, however, one of necessary mediation, but one of antagonism, opening and *risk:* 'the symbol can become subject, value can become command, over-determination can break the dialectic and be in force with power and command' (Negri, 1991: 31).

Money is value; value is money. For Marx, the only route for communism was the destruction of money, the study of money being an important moment in its destruction. Whilst production is premised on exchange-value it is thus impossible to abolish money. This does not mean that the struggle against money is politically irrelevant. As the struggle over the capital relation intensifies it is increasingly directed at money as the most striking and contradictory social form of capital. The problem is that the critique of money must be directed at the social conditions underlying the antagonistic contradictions of money. The crisis of money, therefore, is the crisis of the law of value. Marx uncovered the crisis of social relations which underlies the crisis of money. The limits of the struggle against money are that money is just the perceptible appearance of the contradictory social relations of capital. Furthermore, it is important not to discount the possibility that money has revolutionary potential. However, to focus only on money ignores the way in which the contradictions of money are merely the appearance of the contradictions of the capital relation and that to ignore the capital relation ignores the power of capital to restructure itself in response to the threat of class struggle.

6 The Alien World of Money and Beyond...

The magical qualities of money transfixed the philosophers of the ancient and medieval eras. The quest to turn base metals into gold eluded the greatest of ancient minds. It was the modern bourgeoisie which was to discover the secrets of the philosopher's stone. The class that laid naked the superstitions and chauvinism of the ancient world established themselves as the first great sorcerers in history: a class apparently able to conjure money out of itself through the self-expansion of money. The bourgeoisie solved the mysteries of money and this resulted in the abandonment of philosophical explanations of money. The intellectual representatives of the new magicians established money as an essential component of the natural order and thereby made the philosophical enquiry into its origins and expansion an irrelevant endeavour. Through the work of Adam Smith, David Ricardo and J. S. Mill, money was subsequently reduced to a mere derivative of a rational process of exchange, and the apparent power of money reduced to the powerful rationality of a system based on exchange and mutual equivalence. These writers could not, however, adequately account for the process of accumulation which was a central feature of the emergent capitalist system. The problem was that the working class began to understand and puncture the magical veils behind which the secrets of money were concealed; as the substantive irrationalities and inequalities of capitalist development increasingly undermined the formal rationality of commodity production and exchange. The bourgeoisie perceived the threat and reformulated the magic through the arcane and exotic incantations of marginalist economics and Weberian sociology.

Whilst for classical political economy money emerged as a natural derivative of a rational system, for economists such as Karl Menger and Stanley Jeavons, and sociologists such as

Max Weber and Georg Simmel, money was a derivative of individual action and subjectively interpreted values. The magical separation of the rational (economics) and the irrational (sociology) aspects of this formulation could not, however, withstand the deeply contradictory tendencies contained within money itself. The modern magicians of capital had created a monster that they could no longer control: a monster whose constant transmogrification into ever-greater and more grotesque forms threatened to expose the secret agent lying behind the self-expansion of money: labour. As Marx and Engels noted in the *Communist Manifesto*:

> Modern bourgeois society, a society that has *conjured* up such mighty means of production and exchange, is like a *sorcerer* who can no longer control the powers of the underworld that he has called up by his spells.
>
> (Marx and Engels, 1965: 39; emphasis added)

This threat was the basis on which Keynes was to emerge as 'the last great magician of number'. Keynes recognised the social subjectivity of money through the way in which money evacuated the exchange process in order to maintain itself as a store of value, and the way that this resulted in money being a motive force in determining the crisis-ridden form of capitalist development. The genius of Keynes was his recognition that modern development (modernisation) was premised upon the simultaneous self-expansion of dead labour (objectified in money) and living labour (as subject, personality, as human capital: money). The problem was that Keynes did not recognise the deeply contradictory nature of the form of capital accumulation his work was attempting to understand and rationalise. As Berman (1983) notes, capitalist modernisation is the harnessing of the development (self-expansion) of money-capital and the development (self-expansion) of human individuality and personality. However, the working class exist in, against and through money. Keynesianism had harnessed rather than destroyed the *autonomy* of labour within the institutions of capital. Capital imbued the working class with its own psychological neuroses and irrationalities and called forth the therapy which has become known as *monetarism*. If we are adequately to understand monetarism, we need to explore the intimate connections between the spatial and temporal configurations of capital and the moral and ethical configurations of the self. In the remainder of this chapter, I shall explore the way in which such a project might proceed. I approach this through the concept of *ontology*: an exploration of the relationship between the ontology of capital and the ontology of the self.

ONTOLOGIES OF CAPITAL AND THE SELF

I need to begin with an exploration of the ontological status of capital and the implications of this for the determination of individual identity and subjectivity. I will approach this through an exploration of capital's most ab-stract form – money. Sociology argues that modern money emerged as a consequence of modernity – a tautology which fails to address the specific *form* of money in post-traditional socie-ties (Giddens, 1990, 1991; Dodd, 1994). This is presented as part of the process of time–space distanciation which required the emergence of 'abstract tokens' to mediate social relations ruptured by time and space. The impact of these develop-ments on individual identity was the development of an intensified *reflexivity*: a formulation which stresses the onto-logical differentiation between the self and the forms of social being (i.e. money) through which the self is produced and reproduced. As we have seen, the analysis of money devel-oped by Simmel marks the most developed example of this approach. And yet Simmel also anticipates the postmodern critique of Kantian dualism: the way in which individuals exist through money and define their identities through monet-ary codes and symbols (Lash and Urry, 1994). In other words, money and the self both have a discursive ontological status: the meaning of money defined through processes of intertextuality.

Postmodern writers are right to criticise neo-Kantian analyses of money and usefully highlight the way in which we exist through money as a form of social being. The mistake of this approach is to abstract from the abstract qualities of money in order to produce an abstract theory of money. We must begin with the proposition that money is *real*: money exists as a real social form. As I have shown in the preceding chapters, money developed historically through a real social process of abstraction: money is a real abstraction (rather than an abstract abstraction) and the abstract qualities of money are real. Our own ontological status is also defined by these real abstract qualities: we can only exist through money and our own abstract qualities (our identity and personality) are determined through the same real abstract process. Whilst our subjectivity appears as an abstract categorisation of traits, these are real abstract characteristics because they too are determined through the same real abstract process. Therefore, money and the self share the same ontological status: as a form of social being: an existential categorisation determined through a real abstract historical process.

Modern social science is thus premised on a particular ontological assumption concerning a cognitively grounded conceptualisation of self. Whilst postmodernism is concerned with the decentring and fragmentation of this self, it nevertheless assumes the pre-existence of an ontologically secure self. This is problematic owing to the ambiguity of human existence in time–space. We are simultaneously objectified (alienated) by money and constituted subjectively through money. In a society dominated by money, *I am money*. I am an embodied manifestation of money in all its contradictory manifestations. Money exists simultaneously as C-M-C and M-C-M' and I exist as C-M-C and M-C-M'. True subjectivity is denied by the inner essence of money. Money is the denial of self and the denial of society. In fact, money is society and money is the self. There is no reality (objective or subjective) outside the reality of money. Human society is constituted as the alien power which infests and colonises the inner-life of man and which denies the possibility of society except through the alien society of money. Money is the universal whore through which I prostitute my humanity. Humanity, however, is no more than an abstraction created by the abstract power of money. Money simultaneously invented humanity and denied humanity. Humanity becomes a cyborg: an automaton denied existence by the alien which infests her life-world.

THE LAND OF THE CYBORGS: BEYOND THE ALIEN PLANET OF LABOUR

In Marxist science the notion of the relation between man and machine (cybernetics) is investigated through the concept of alienated labour. Whilst the process through which alienation occurs is the subject of much debate, the category labour is not addressed. Incredibly, labour is the last great unexplored region of Marxist scholarship. Whilst the category of labour is taken on uncritically in liberal social science, e.g. economics, industrial relations and management studies, the focus within Marxism has tended to be on the activity of workers forming collective associations at work: trade unions. But labour demands attention. Now more than ever. The programme that identified labour with worker has been corrupted by an anti-virus: desire.

This anti-virus appeared in a virulent form in the worker struggles of the early 1960s throughout Europe and most articulately in the 'Autonomia' movement in Northern Italy. Autonomia was both an intensely practical and a theoretical project, concerned with the organisation of worker resistance and the position of theory (intellectuals) within that process. Through a science of subversion it sought, by focusing on the capital/labour dynamic, (the capital relation) to invert the class perspective and so examine the capital relation from the position of labour. Autonomist intellectuals (Negri, Tronti) argued that changes in the organic composition of capital, the replacement of variable capital (labour) by constant capital (machines), were not motivated by the logic of capital but were the result of the inability of capital to subordinate labour to the imperatives of valorisation. The changes imposed by labour forced capital to recompose itself and decompose labour. This recomposition does not resolve anything, but rather, provides the basis for further struggles. As these struggles develop they move outside the workplace to contaminate the whole of human life. Civilisation is organised as 'one vast labour camp – the global Gulag' (Cleaver, 1992: 116). But despite this real subsumption of labour by capital, resistance continues as 'self-valorisation': the creative use of time and space as multiple counter-cultures leading to the creation of autonomous subjectivities.

> Now that the class struggle is over the whole social working day and is being waged by a fully socialised proletariat, it is impossible to see relations of production merely as a by-product or 'result' of production relations: the contemporary crisis of capitalism requires a further social dimension beyond the workerist analysis of the 60s and 70s – the crisis is both a crisis of production and of the reproduction of wage work relations as a whole.
>
> (Negri, 1988: 177)

Despite the importance of this exposition the Autonomists failed to explain labour in terms of the crisis of work relations as a whole. Capital is presented as if it were an extra-human thing and labour a human thing, rather than labour as an extra-human thing and capital as what humans are. The Autonomists presented labour as a form of existence that was independent of capital, rather than as a form of social existence that has been formed, or perverted, by capital as alienated labour. Whilst they understood the process of alienation, the real existence of labour had not been explained. If capital is alienated labour, then labour cannot be independent. It can only be understood as labour's constitutive power in a mode of being denied in the capitalist form of social reproduction (Bonefeld, 1994: 49–50).

This immanence suggests a more intimate relation between man and machine than has formally been acknowledged in

Marxist scholarship. As the distinction between body and machine becomes indistinguishable, the importance of a communist science of the cyborg becomes more compelling (Hardt and Negri, 1995). At the present moment technical and intellectual labour is tending towards abstract and immaterial, complex and cooperative processes. All this is intensified by the appearance of the computer in its digital and DNA (human) form. The machine is now integral to the subject and not just an appendage, as it was for Marx. The subject is both human and machine throughout its core, its nature: there is a new human nature coursing through our bodies. Postmodernism is right, the subject has disappeared; postmodernism is wrong, the subject has been replaced by a new subject, the cyborg, who as subjectivity is the affirmation of life who is communism:

> The contradiction of exploitation is thus displaced onto a very high level, where the subject who is principally exploited is recognized in its creative subjectivity but controlled in the management of the power that it expresses. It is from this very high point of command that the contradiction spills over into the entire society. And it is therefore with respect to this very high point of command that the entire social horizon of exploitation tends to unify, situating within the antagonistic relationship all the elements of self-valorisation at whichever level they arise.
>
> (Hardt and Negri, 1995: 281)

Man is not simply the bearer of a relation or an appendage to the machine. Man is the relation. He is the machine. There is nothing else. In this cybernetic universe machines and the logic of machines (production) have replaced man and nature. Nothing else has any meaning, everything is production, everything has the same essential reality, with desire (antivirus) as its immanent principle; its divine energy dissolving all idealistic and normative categories.

It is at work everywhere, functioning smoothly at times, at other times in fits and starts. It breathes, it heats, it eats. It shits and fucks. What a mistake to have ever said the id. Everywhere it is machines – real ones, not figurative ones: machines driving other machines, with all the necessary couplings and connections. An organ-machine is plugged into an energy-source machine: the one produces a flow that the other interrupts. The breast is a machine that produces milk, and the mouth a machine coupled to it. The mouth of the anorexic wavers between several functions: its possessor is uncertain as to whether it an eating-machine, an anal machine, a talking machine or a breathing machine (asthma attacks)...

(Deleuze and Guattari, 1984: 1)

The machine will not take over the world in the immediate future. It already has. Human labour is not an appendage to the machine, it is the machine. The world is labour. The world is a machine. There is, then, a connection between the empirical reality described by liberal social science and this cyborg science: labour is invisible because labour is everything. In order to avoid this overwhelming abstraction, we need to become travellers in time and space. The space and time we need to explore is not, however, the inter-galactic world of outer-space but the hidden and alien inner-spaces infested by the grotesque and perverted forms of money-capital. There is another world concealed within the world: i.e. the world of sustainable life, communism – the science of the future.

Notes

1 MONEY CHANGES EVERYTHING...

1. For an exploration of 'open Marxism', see the collection of essays presented in Bonefeld et al. (1991a, 1991b, 1995).
2. See Clarke (1991b), Bonefeld and Holloway (1991), Bonefeld et al. (1992a, 1992b, 1995) and Mohun (1994) for collections of essays espousing this form of 'open' Marxism.

3 RISKY BUSINESS! THE CRISIS OF INSURANCE AND THE LAW OF LOTTERY

1. We would like to thank our friend William Dixon for providing historical and theoretical insights into the significance of William Beveridge to the development of state welfare insurance.
2. This is evident in Giddens's institutionalist approach to the analysis of modern societies. Giddens argues that modern political and economic institutions are 'bounded' but his own structural functionalist methodology precludes an assessment of the dynamics through which boundaries are developed and sustained. See Giddens (1985: 294–341).
3. Lash and Urry argue that both value and use-value were 'abstract' in the modern age and have both been transplanted by 'sign value' in the post-modern age (Lash and Urry, 1994: 14). Similarly, Foucauldian writers allude to the 'capitalization of everyday life' and the constitution of individual subjectivity through discursive projects of enterprise and money (Foucault, 1991; Rose, 1989).

4 PROBATION, CRIMINOLOGY AND ANTI-OPPRESSION

1. Valorisation is the process by which capital expands itself, expressed in the equation: $M-C-M'-C-M''$.
2. I highlighted the revolutionary potential of Keynes's theory of money in chapter 2.

3. In his book, Hill records the alternative forms of existence (communal property, radical democracy, struggles against the Protestant work ethic) that were being lived in opposition to the dominant money form (e.g. Levellers, Ranters, Diggers), oppositions that were to be subsumed within the logic of monetised society. These alternatives have not been eradicated.

Bibliography

Aglietta, M. (1979) *A Theory of Capitalist Regulation: The US Experience*, London, Verso.

Appadurai, A. (1990) 'Disjuncture and Difference in the Global Cultural Economy', in M. Featherstone (ed.), *Global Culture*, London, Sage.

Bahlman, D. (1968) *The Moral Revolution of 1688*, Hamden, Conn., Archon Books.

Baudrillard, J. (1968) *Le Système des objects*, Paris, Denoël-Gonthier.

Baudrillard, J. (1978) *La Société de consommation*, Paris, Gallimard.

Baudrillard, J. (1981) *For a Critique of the Political Economy of the Sign*, St Louis, Telos Press.

Bauman, Z. (1991) *Modernity and Ambivalence*, Cambridge, Polity.

Beck, U. (1992) *Risk Society: Towards a New Modernity*, London, Sage.

Beck, U. (1995) *Ecological Politics in the Age of Risk*, London, Sage.

Becker, G. (1962) 'Investment in Human Capital: A Theoretical Approach', *Journal of Political Economy*, No. 5.

Berman, M. (1983) *All That is Solid Melts into Air: The Experience of Modernity*, London, Verso.

Bologna, S. (1993) 'Money and Crisis: Marx as Correspondent of the *New York Daily Tribune*', *Common Sense*, 13/14.

Bonefeld, W. (1992) 'Social Constitution and the Form of the Capitalist State', in W. Bonefeld, R. Gunn and K. Pyschopedis (eds), *Open Marxism: Dialectics and History*, London, Pluto Press.

Bonefeld, W. (1993) *The Recomposition of the British State During the 1980s*, Aldershot, Dartmouth.

Bonefeld, W. (1994) 'Human Practice and Perversion: Beyond Autonomy and Structure', in *Common Sense*, No. 15.

Bonefeld, W. (1995) 'Capital as Subject and the Existence of Labour', in W. Bonefeld, R. Gunn, J. Holloway, and K. Pyschopedis (eds), *Open Marxism: Emancipating Marx*, London, Pluto Press.

Bonefeld, W. (1996) 'Money, Equality and Exploitation: an Interpretation of Marx's treatment of Money', in W. Bonefeld and J. Holloway (eds), *Global Capital, National State and the Politics of Money*, London, Macmillan.

Bonefeld, W. and Holloway, J. (eds) (1991) *Post-Fordism and Social Form: a Marxist Debate on the Post-Fordist State*, London, Macmillan.

Bonefeld, W., Gunn, R. and Pyschopedis, K. (eds) (1992a) *Open Marxism: Dialectics and History*, London, Pluto Press.
Bonefeld, W., Gunn, R. and Pyschopedis, K. (eds) (1992b) *Open Marxism: Theory and Practice*, London, Pluto Press.
Bonefeld, W., Gunn, R. Holloway, J. and Pyschopedis, K. (eds) (1995) *Open Marxism: Emancipating Marx*, London, Pluto Press.
Bourdieu, P. (1984) *Distinction: A Social Critique of the Judgement of Taste*, London, Routledge.
Bromley, S. (1991) 'The Politics of Postmodernism', *Capital and Class*, No. 45.
Burnham, P. (1990) *The Political Economy of Postwar Reconstruction*, London, Macmillan.
Burnham, P. (1991) 'Neo-Gramscian Hegemony and the International State System', *Capital & Class*, No. 45.
Burnham, P. (1996) 'Capital, Crisis and the International State System', in W. Bonefeld and J. Holloway (eds) *Global Capital, National State and the Politics of Money*, London, Macmillan.
Camelot (1996) *Annual Report and Accounts*, Camelot Group Plc, Watford.
Clarke, S. (1988) *Money, the State and the Illusory Community*, unpublished working paper.
Clarke, S. (1991a) *Marx, Marginalism and Modern Sociology: From Adam Smith to Max Weber*, London, Macmillan.
Clarke, S. (ed.) (1991b) *The State Debate*, London, Macmillan.
Clarke, S. (1994) *Marx's Theory of Crisis*, London, Macmillan.
Cleaver, H. (1979) *Reading Capital Politically*, Brighton, Harvester Press.
Cleaver, H. (1992) 'The Inversion of Class Perspective in Marxian Theory: From Valorisation to Self-Valorisation', in W. Bonefeld, R. Gunn, and K. Pyschopedis (eds), *Open Marxism: Theory and Practice*, London, Pluto Press.
Craig, J. (1946) *Newton at the Mint*, Cambridge, Cambridge University Press.
Croakley, J. and Harris, L. (1983) *The City of Capital*, Oxford, Blackwell.
Crosland, M.P. (1962) *Historical Studies in the Language of Chemistry*, London, Heinemann.
Curtis, T.C. and Speck, W.A. (1976) 'The Societies for the Reformation of Manners: a Case Study in the Theory and Practice of Moral Reform', *Literature and History*, No. 3, March.
Debord, G. (1977) *The Society of the Spectacle*, Detroit, Black and Red.
Defoe, D. (1978) *Moll Flanders*, London, Penguin Books.
Deleuze, G. and Guattari, F. (1984) *Anti-Oedipus: Capitalism and Schizophrenia*, London, Athlone Press.

Derrida, J. (1992) *Given Time: 1. Counterfeit Money*, Chicago, University of Chicago Press.

Derrida, J. (1994) 'Spectres of Marx', *New Left Review*, No. 205, May/June.

Dixon, W. (1996) *The Development of the Concept of Unemployment Leading to Keynes's General Theory*, unpublished PhD Thesis, City University, London.

Dobb, B. (1975) *The Foundations of Newton's Alchemy*, Cambridge, Cambridge University Press.

Dodd, N. (1994) *The Sociology of Money: Economics, Reason and Contemporary Society*, Cambridge, Polity.

Dodd, N. (1995) *The Sociology of Money: Questions of Trust and Risk* 'Sociology and the Limits of Economics Conference', University of Liverpool, 20–22 April.

Featherstone, M. (1991) *Consumer Culture and Postmodernism*, London, Sage.

Fine, R. (1984) *Democracy and the Rule of Law*, London, Pluto Press.

Fischer, E. (1978) *A Marxist Approach*, trans. A. Bostock, London, Penguin Books.

Fitzherbert, L., Gussani, C. and Hurd, H. (1996) *The National Lottery Yearbook*, London, Directory of Social Change.

Foucault, M. (1991) 'Politics and the Study of Discourse' and 'Governmentability', in G. Burchill, C. Gordon and P. Miller (eds) *The Foucault Effect: Studies in Governmentability*, London, Harvester Wheatsheaf.

Friere, P. (1993) *The Pedagogy of the Oppressed*, Harmondsworth, Penguin.

Fromm, E. (1971) *The Crisis of Psychoanalysis: Essays on Freud, Marx and Social Psychology*, London, Jonathan Cape.

Giddens, A. (1985) *The Nation State and Violence: Volume Two of a Contemporary Critique of Historical Materialism*, Berkeley and Los Angeles, University of California Press.

Giddens, A. (1990) *The Consequences of Modernity*, Cambridge, Polity.

Giddens, A. (1991) *Modernity and Self-Identity: Self and Society in the Late Modern Age*, Cambridge, Polity.

Graef, R. (1993) *Living Dangerously*, London, HarperCollins.

Granovetter, M. and Swedberg, R. (eds) (1992) *The Sociology of Economic Life*, Boulder, Westview Press.

Habermas, J. (1972) *Knowledge and Human Interests*, London, Heinemann.

Habermas, J. (1984) *Reason and the Rationalization of Society*, London, Heinemann.

Habermas, J. (1987) *The Theory of Communicative Action: Volume Two. Lifeworld and System: A Critique of Functionalist Reason*, Cambridge, Polity.

Habermas, J. (1988) *Legitimation Crisis*, Cambridge, Polity.

Hardt, M. and Negri, A. (1995) *Labour of Dionysis: A Critique of the State Form*, Minneapolis, University of Minnesota Press.

Harvey, D. (1990) *The Condition of Postmodernity*, Oxford, Blackwell.

Haxby, D. (1978) *Probation: a Changing Service*, London, Macmillan.

Heller, A. (1974) *The Theory of Need in Marx*, London, Allison & Busby.

Hill, C. (1977) *Reformation to Industrial Revolution*, Harmondsworth, Penguin.

Hill, C. (1991) *The World Turned Upside Down: Radical Ideas during the English Revolution*, Harmondsworth, Penguin.

Holloway, J. and Picciotto, S. (1991) 'Capital, Crisis and the State', in S. Clarke (ed.), *The State Debate*, London, Macmillan.

Ingham, G. (1996) 'Some Recent Changes in the Relationship Between Economics and Sociology', *Cambridge Journal of Economics*, Vol. 20, pp. 243–75.

Jameson, F. (1991) *Postmodernism Or, the Cultural Logic of Late Capitalism*, London, Verso.

Kay, G. and Mott, J. (1982) *Political Order and the Law of Labour*, London, Macmillan.

Keynes, J. M. (1973) *The General Theory of Employment, Interest and Money*, London, Macmillan.

Lacan, J. (1966) *Écrits*, Paris, Le Seuil.

Laing, R. D. (1990) *The Divided Self: an Existential Study in Sanity and Madness*, Harmondsworth, Penguin Books.

Lang, P. (1994) *Lets Work: Rebuilding the Local Economy*, Bristol, Grover Books.

Lash, S. (1990) *The Sociology of Postmodernism*, London, Routledge.

Lash, S. and Urry, J. (1987) *The End of Organised Capitalism*, Cambridge: Polity.

Lash, S. and Urry, J. (1994) *Economies of Signs and Space*, London, Sage.

Lee, R. (1996) 'Moral Money? Lets and the Social Construction of Local Economic Geographies in South East England', *Environment and Planning* Vol. 28, No. 8.

Linebaugh, P. (1991) *The London Hanged: Crime and Civil Society in the 18th Century*, London, Allen Lane/Penguin Books.

Linton, M. (1996) 'Local Currency', in P. Ekins (ed.) *The Living Economy: A New Economics in the Making*, London, Routledge.

London–Edinburgh Weekend Return Group (1979) *In and Against the State*, London, Pluto Press.

Lukács, G. (1971) *History and Class Consciousness: Studies in Marxist Dialectics*, London, Merlin.

MacIntyre, A. (1981) *After Virtue*, London, Duckworth.

MacIntyre, A. (1988) *Whose Justice? Which Rationality?*, London, Duckworth.

MacWilliams, W. (1987) 'Probation, Pragmatism and Policy', *The Howard Journal*, Vol. 26, No. 2, May.

Maffesoli, M. (1991) *Les Temps de tribus: le déclin de l'individualisme dans les sociétés de masse*, Paris, Livre de Poche.

Marx, K. (1954) *Capital: A Critique of Political Economy. Vol. One*, London, Lawrence & Wishart.

Marx, K. (1956a) 'Comments on Adolf Wagner', in *Werke* Vol. 19, pp. 355ff, Berlin.

Marx, K. (1956b) *Capital Volume Two: The Process of Circulation of Capital*, London, Lawrence and Wishart.

Marx, K. (1959) *Capital Volume Three: The Process of Capitalist Production as a Whole*, London, Lawrence and Wishart.

Marx, K. (1971a) *Theories of Surplus Value: Volume Three*, Moscow, Progress Publishers.

Marx, K. (1971b) *A Contribution to the Critique of Political Economy*, London, Lawrence and Wishart.

Marx, K. (1973) *Grundrisse: Foundations of the Critique of Political Economy*, London, Allen Lane.

Marx, K. (1975a) 'Excerpts from James Mill's *Elements of Political Economy*', in *Early Writings* Harmondsworth, Penguin Books.

Marx, K. (1975b) 'Economic and Philosophical Manuscripts', in *Early Writings* Harmondsworth, Penguin Books.

Marx, K. (1976) *Capital: A Critique of Political Economy*, Harmondsworth, Penguin Books.

Marx, K. and Engels, F. (1965) *Manifesto of the Communist Party*, Peking, Foreign Language Press.

Marx, K. and Engels, F. (1974) *The German Ideology*, London, Lawrence and Wishart.

Mattick, P. (1971) *Marx and Keynes: The Limits of the Mixed Economy*, London, Merlin.

Mauss, M. (1969) *Elementary Structures of Kinship*, Boston, Beacon Press.

May, T. (1994) 'Under Siege: the Probation Service in a Changing Environment', in R. Reiner and M. Cross (eds) *Beyond Law and Order, Criminal Justice Policy and Politics in the 1990s*, London, Macmillan.

Melucci, A. (1989) *Nomads of the Present*, London, Hutchinson, Radius.

Miliband, R. (1969) *The State in Capitalist Society*, London, Weidenfeld & Nicolson.

Miliband, R. (1973) 'The Capitalist State', *New Left Review* No. 59.

Mitchell, J. (1978) Introduction to D. Defoe, *Moll Flanders*, Harmondsworth, Penguin Books.

Mohun, S. (ed.) (1994) *Debates in Value Theory*, London, Macmillan.

More, T. (1989) *Utopia*, in A. Robin, *A History of Economic Thought*, London.

Nader, R. (1992) *Time Dollars*, Emmaus, Rodale Press.

Negri, A. (1988) *Revolution Retrieved: Selected Writings on Marx, Keynes, Capitalist Crisis & New Social Subjects 1967–83*, London, Red Notes.

Negri, A. (1991) *Marx beyond Marx: Lessons on the Grundrisse*, London, Pluto Press.

Nellis, M. (1995) 'Probation Values for the 1990s', *The Howard Journal* Vol. 34, No. 1, February.

Offe, C. and Heinze, R. (1992) *Beyond Employment: Time, Work and the Informal Economy*, Cambridge, Polity.

Parsons, T. (1951) *The Social System*, London, Tavistock.

Parsons, T. and Smelser, N. J. (1956) *Economy and Society: A Study in the Integration of Economic and Social Theory*, London, Routledge and Kegan Paul.

Pashukanis, E. B. (1978) *Law and Marxism: A General Theory* London, Pluto Press.

Poulantzas, N. (1969) 'The Problem of the Capitalist State', *New Left Review*, No. 58.

Poulantzas, N. (1973) *Political Power and Social Classes*, London, New Left Books.

Radzinowicz, L. (1948/1956) *The History of English Criminal Law and its Administration from 1750*, Vols 1, 2 & 3, London, Stevens.

Read, J. (1961) *Through Alchemy to Chemistry*, London, Bell and Sons.

Reich, W. (1968) *The Function of the Orgasm*, London, Panther.

Reich, W. (1970) *The Mass Psychology of Fascism*, New York, Farrar Strauss and Giroux.

Rosdolsky, R. (1980) *The Making of Marx's Capital: Volume One*, London, Pluto Press.

Rose, N. (1989) *Governing the Soul: Technologies of Human Subjectivity*, London, Routledge.

Rousseau, J-J. (1973) *The Social Contract and Discourses*, London, Dent & Sons.

Rubin, I. I. (1973) *Essays on Marx's Theory of Value*, Montreal, Black Rose Books.

Rubin, I. I. (1979) *A History of Economic Thought*, London, Pluto Press.

Rustin, M. (1994) 'A Review of "Risk Society: Towards a New Modernity" by Ulrich Beck', *Radical Philosophy*, No. 66.

Sallnow, J. (1994) 'LETS go to Work', *Geographical*, May.

Samuelson, P. A. (1967) *Economics: An Introductory Analysis*, New York, McGraw-Hill.

Schumpeter, J. A. (1987) *Capitalism, Socialism and Democracy*, London, Unwin.

Sève, L. (1975) *Marxism and the Theory of Human Personality*, London, Lawrence and Wishart.

Skiddelsky, R. (1986) *John Maynard Keynes, A Biography: Vol. 1. Hopes Betrayed 1883–1920*, London, Viking.

Skiddelsky, R. (1992) *John Maynard Keynes, A Biography: Vol. 2. The Economist as Saviour 1920–1937*, London, Macmillan.

Smith, A. (1970) *The Wealth of Nations*, Harmondsworth, Penguin Books.

Taylor, C. (1989) *Sources of the Self: The Making of Modern Identity*, Cambridge, Cambridge University Press.

Thompson, E. P. (1968) *The Making of the English Working Class*, Harmondsworth, Pelican.

Thompson, E. P. (1977) *Whigs and Hunters*, Harmondsworth, Penguin Books.

Thompson, E. P. (1978) *The Poverty of Theory and Other Essays*, London, Merlin.

Tourraine, A. (1982) *The Voice and the Eye*, Cambridge, Cambridge University Press.

Tully, J. (1982) *A Discourse on Property: John Locke and His Adversaries*, Cambridge, Cambridge University Press.

Walzer, M. (1983) *Spheres of Justice*, New York, Basic Books.

Weber, M. (1968) *Economy and Society*, 3 volumes, Berkeley, University of California Press.

Wiggerhaus, R. (1994) *The Frankfurt School: Its History, Theories and Political Significance*, trans. M. Robinson, Cambridge, Polity Press.

Willett, A. H. (1951) *The Economic Theory of Risk and Insurance*, Philadelphia, University of Pennsylvania Press.

Williams, C. C. (1996) 'Informal Sector Responses to Unemployment: An Evaluation of the Potential of LETS', *Work, Employment and Society*, Vol. 10, No. 2.

Index